ISBN: 9781407674391

Published by:
HardPress Publishing
8345 NW 66TH ST #2561
MIAMI FL 33166-2626

Email: info@hardpress.net
Web: http://www.hardpress.net

Feb   8

69640

Very faithfully your
Kanzō Uchimura.

THE DIARY

OF A JAPANESE CONVERT

BY KANZŌ UCHIMURA

ENCOURAGEMENT:

"Veracity, true simplicity of heart, how valuable are these always!
He that speaks what is really in him, will find men to listen, though
under never such impediments."—THOMAS CARLYLE.

FLEMING H. REVELL COMPANY

NEW YORK   CHICAGO   TORONTO

Tokyo, Japan : Keiseisha : Idzumocho, Kyobashiku

*   *   *   *   *   *

I am grateful to you for sending me the advance sheets of this wonderful book, for it is a wonderful book. It is an interpretative study which a man makes of himself in life's crises and in the more serious periods of his career. It has visions of truth such as are given to but few to see. It also has a vital element in every part, which grips one to the book with tremendous fixedness.

I shall be interested to know whether the thinking people of America wake up to the presence among themselves of a book of this character.

What a satisfaction it is to come into close relations with a mighty mind! Most of us human beings are fitted for only a common life. Of course "God likes common people," as it is said, "or He would not have made so many of us," but after all I am sure that he prefers the nobly uncommon, and we ourselves certainly like the uncommon and conspicuous.

CHAS. F. THWING,

President of Western Reserve University, Cleveland, Ohio.

I am glad that this heart experience of a Japanese is to be given to the public in America. It is suggestive, instructive and valuable in many ways. No one can read it without realizing more fully the strength of Christianity, and that its strength is in the living Christ himself, who dwells with the soul who will receive Him.

I am glad that this picture is given of the outcome of the year of work which President Clark did in Sapporo, as he helped to organize the Agricultural College there, and insisted that the Bible should be taken as the basis of the morality taught in the institution. The little band of believers whom he left there have held on through more than twenty years, almost every one of them a tower of strength in Japan.

I am glad of this tribute to the noble heart of President Seelye, of Amherst, as well as for the words (in general just) of criticism, favorable and unfavorable, upon our American Christianity, and upon foreign missions.   J. D. DAVIS,

Of Doshisha University, Kyoto, Japan, and Author of "Life of Nescima,"
October, 1895.

TO ALL THE GOODLY SOULS
WHO APPEAR IN THESE PAGES BY THEIR
INITIALS AND OTHERWISE,
AS GOD-SENT MESSENGERS TO PREPARE MY
SOUL FOR HEAVEN,
THIS HUMBLE DESCRIPTION OF THE
CHIEFEST OF SINNERS
IS MOST AFFECTIONATELY
DEDICATED.

NOTE.

This Book by a native Japanese, written in English by himself, from his Japanese home, will, we believe, be acceptable to a wide circle of American readers. So far as we know, it is the only book of the kind ever published in any language ; and as a vivid portraiture of a struggling soul seeking light and peace for his and his nation's salvation, it will be read with deep interest by all who desire the good of humanity. It touches upon many vital questions connected with Christian missions in "heathen" lands ; and written in autobiographical form, it has all the freshness and reality of the author's own actual experiences.

Except in a few instances when the meaning might not have been quite clear, the work is issued as written by the author. The occasional indications of a foreign idiom but enhances the reader's interest, and it was not thought best to alter these or critically correct every minor inaccurate form of expression as judged by our English usage.

PREFACE.

In many a religious gathering to which I was invited during my stay in America to give a talk for fifteen minutes and no more (as some great doctor, the chief speaker of the meeting, was to fill up the most of the time). I often asked the chairman (or the chairwoman) what they would like to hear from me. The commonest answer I received was, "O just tell us how you were converted." I was always at a loss how to comply with such a demand, as I could not in any way tell in "fifteen minutes and no more" the awful change that came over my soul since I was brought in contact with Christianity. The fact is, the conversion of a heathen is always a matter of wonder, if not of curiosity, to the Christian public; and it was just natural that I too was asked to tell them some vivid accounts of how "I threw my idols into the fire, and clung unto the Gospel." But mine was a more obdurate case than those of many other converts. Though moments of ecstacy and sudden spiritual illuminations were not wanting, my conversion was a slow gradual process. I was not converted in a day. Long after I ceased to prostrate myself before idols, yea long after I was baptized, I lacked those beliefs in the fundamental teachings of Christianity which I now consider to be essential in calling myself a Christian. Even yet "I count not myself to have apprehended"; and as I press toward the mark for the prize of the high calling of God in Christ Jesus, I know

not whether I may yet find my present position
to be still heathenish. These pages are the honest confessions of the various stages of the
spiritual growth I have passed through. Will
the reader receive them as the unadorned ex-
pressions of a human heart, and judge with
leniency the language in which they are written,
as it is not the tongue that I learned from my
mother's lips, and the ornate literature is not the
trade by which I live in this world.   K. U.
An Isle in the Pacific.
    May 1, 1895.

CONTENTS.

DIARY OF A JAPANESE CONVERT.

INTRODUCTION.

I propose to write how I became a Christian and not why. The so-called "philosophy of conversion" is not my theme. I will only describe its "phenomena," and will furnish materials for more disciplined minds than mine to philosophize upon. I early contracted the habit of keeping my diary, in which I noted down whatever ideas and events came to pass upon me. I made myself a subject of careful observations, and found it more mysterious than anything I ever have studied. I jotted down its rise and progress, its falls and backslidings, its joys and hopes, its sins and darkness; and notwithstanding all the awfulness that attends such an observation like this, I found it more seriously interesting than any study I ever have undertaken. I call my diary a "log-book," as a book in which is entered the daily progress of this poor bark toward the upper haven through sins, and tears, and many a woe. I might just as well call it a "biologist's sketch-book," in which is kept the accounts of all the morphological and physiological changes of a soul in its embryological development from a seed to a full-eared corn. A part of such a record is now given to the

public, and the reader may draw whatever con-
clusions he likes from it. My diary, however,
begins only a few months before I accepted
Christianity.

CHAPTER I.

HEATHENISM

I was born, according to the Gregorian calendar, on the 28th of March, 1861. My family belonged to the warrior class; so I was born to fight— *vivere est militare,*—from the very cradle. My paternal grandfather was every-inch a soldier. He was never so happy as when he appeared in his ponderous armour, decked with a bamboo-bow and pheasant-feathered arrows and a 50-pound fire-lock. He lamented that the land was in peace, and died with regret that he never was able to put his trade in practice. My father was more cultured, could write good poetry, and was learned in the art of ruling man. He too was a man of no mean military ability, and could lead a most turbulent regiment in a very creditable way.—Maternally, my grandfather was essentially an honest man. Indeed he had few other abilities than honesty, if honesty could be called an ability in this glorious selfish century. It is told of him that when he was asked to lend out some public money with usury-interest (a custom very common with treasurers of petty provincial lords, who of course pocketed the whole of the interest money), my grandfather was too wise to offend his head-officers by disobeying them, but was too conscientious to exact exorbitant rates from the poor borrowers; so he kept the money with him, and at the expiration of the term, he returned it to the usurious officers, with high interest upon it out of his own pocket. He also was a total abstainer. I do not believe more than twenty cups of fiery drinks ever passed his lips in his life-time, and this only by the recommendation of his doctors.—My maternal grandmother was a worthy companion to this honest and abstemious man. She was born to work,— *vivere est laborare* for her,—and for forty years she did work as any frail human being could work. For fifty years she lived a life of widowhood, brought up and educated five children with her own hands, never proved false to her neighbor, never ran in debt; and now in her four-scores-and-four, with her ears closed to the noise and din of the world, her deep eyes ever bathed with tears, she calmly waits for the shadow to relieve her from the life she so bravely fought through. A pathos there is in "heathenism" so noble as hers. She is too sacred to be touched with the hand of inexperience whatever theologies and philosophies it can handle. Let the Spirit of God alone mould her, and no ill shall come to her well-tried soul.* My mother has inherited from her mother this mania for work. She forgets all the pains and sorrows of life in her work. She is one of those who "can't afford" to be gloomy because life is hard. Her little home is her kingdom, and she rules it, washes it, feeds it, as no queen has ever done.

Such was my parentage, and such were the hearts which moulded me. But to no one of them do I trace the origin of my "religious sensibilities" which I early acquired in my boyhood. My father

---

* She passed away in peace during the preparation of this book.

was decidedly blasphemous toward heathen gods of all sorts. He once dropped a base coin into the money-chest of a Buddhist temple, and scornfully addressed the idols there that they would have another such coin if they would in any way help him to win a law-case in which he was then engaged;—a feat wholly beyond my power at any period of my religious experience. But I always thank my God that I never have tasted human flesh, or prostrated myself before the wheels of Juggernaut, or witnessed infants fed to gavials. If in my childhood I had no blessed Sabbath home to draw upward my secret heart with influence sweet, I was spared much of mammonism, of the fearful curse of rum-traffic, so common in other *doms* than heathendoms. If there were no Gospel stories to calm down my childish passion's rage, that excitement and rush of the so-called Christendom which whirls men and women into premature graves was unknown to me. If heathenism is the reign of darkness, it is the reign of moon and stars, of obscure lights no doubt, but withal of repose and comparative innocence.

My father was a good Confucian scholar, who could repeat from memory almost every passage in the writings and sayings of the sage. So naturally my early education was in that line; and though I could not understand the ethico-political precepts of the Chinese sages, I was imbued with the general sentiments of their teachings. Loyality to my feudal lords, and fidelity and respects to my parents and teachers, were the central themes of the Chinese ethics. Filial piety was taught to be the source of all virtues, akin to the Solomonic precept of "Fear of God is the beginning of wisdom." The story of a filial youth responding to an unreasonable demand of an old parent to have a tender bamboo-shoot (the asparagus of the Orient) at midwinter, of his search for it in forest, and of its miraculous sprout from under the snow is as vivid to the memory of every child in my land as the story of Joseph to that of every Christian youth. Even parental tyranny and oppression were to be meekly borne, and many illustrations were cited from the deeds of ancient worthies in this respect.—Loyality to feudal lords, especially in time of war, took more romantic shapes in the ethical conceptions of the youth of my land. He was to consider his life as light as dust when called to serve his lord in exigency; and the noblest spot where he could die was in front of his master's steed, thrice blessed if his corpse was trampled under its hoof. —No less weightier was to be the youth's consideration for his master (his intellectual and moral preceptor), who was to him no mere school-teacher or college professor on *quid pro quo* principle, but a veritable didaskalos, in whom he could and must completely confide the care of his body and soul. The Lord, the Father, and the Master, constituted his Trinity. Neither one of them was inferior to any other in his consideration, and the most vexing question to him was which he would save, if the three of them were on the point of drowning at the same time, and he had ability to save but one. Then, their enemies were to be his own enemies, with whom he was not allowed to bear the same benignant heaven. These were to be pursued even to the very ends of the earth, and satisfaction must be had, eye for eye, tooth for tooth.

Strong in inculcating obedience and reverence toward our superiors, the oriental precepts are

not wanting in regard to our relations to our
equals and inferiors. Sincerity in friendship.
harmony in brotherhood, and leniency toward
the inferior and the governed are strongly
insisted upon. Much reported cruelties of
heathens toward women do not find encouragement to that effect in their moral code,
neither is it entirely silent upon the subject. Our
ideal mothers and wives and sisters are not very
inferior to the conception of the highest Christian
womanhood, and the very fact that some of them
achieved high excellence in deeds and character
without the exalting influence of Christianity
makes me to admire them so much more.

Side by side with these and other instructions,
not inferior, I sincerely believe, to those which are
imparted to, and possessed by, many who call
themselves Christians, I was not free from many
drawbacks and much superstition.

The most defective point in Chinese ethics is
its weakness when it deals with sexual morality.
Not that it is wholly silent upon the virtue of
social purity, but the way in which the violation
of the law of chastity is usually dealt with, and
its connivance upon the perpetrators of the same,
resulted in general apathy in this respect. Polygamy in its strict sense has never entered into
oriental minds; but concubinage, which amounts
to the same thing, has met only mildest rebukes,
if any, from their moralists. Amidst solemn instructions of my father about duty and high
ambition, I discerned words of emulation for
study and industry with an opulent harem in view.
Great statesmanship and learning may exist without ideas of chastity. He that grasps the rein of
the state in sober hours may rest upon a bosom
of uncleanliness in less serious moments. Glar-

ing profligacy does often attend acute intellect and high regard for public honor, and though I am not blind to darkness as great in other countries than my own, I do not hesitate in attributing impotence to Chinese ethics when it deals with questions of social purity.

But no retrospect of my bygone days causes in me a greater humiliation than the spiritual darkness I groped under, laboriously sustained with gross superstitions. I believed, and that sincerely, that there dwelt in each of innumerable temples its god, jealous over its jurisdiction, ready with punishment to any transgressor that fell under his displeasure. The god whom I reverenced and adored most was the god of learning and writing, for whom I faithfully observed the 25th of every month with due sanctity and sacrifice. I prostrated myself before his image, earnestly implored his aid to improve my handwriting and help my memory. Then there is a god who presides over rice-culture, and his errands unto mortals are white foxes. He can be approached with prayers to protect our houses from fire and robbery, and as my father was mostly away from home, and I was alone with my mother, I ceased not to beseech this god of rice to keep my poor home from the said disasters. There was another god whom I feared more than all others. His emblem was a black raven, and he was the searcher of man's inmost heart. The keeper of his temple issued papers upon which ravens were printed in sombre colors, the whole having a miraculous property to cause immediate hemorrage when taken into stomach by any one who told falsehood. I often vindicated my truthfulness before my comrades by calling upon them to test my veracity by the use of a piece of this sacred paper, if they stood in suspicion of what I asserted. Still another god exercises healing power upon those who suffer from toothache. Him also did I call upon, as I was a constant sufferer from this painful malady. He would exact from his devotee a vow to abstain from pears as specially obnoxious to him, and I was of course most willing to undergo the required privation. Future study in Chemistry and Toxicology revealed to me a good scientific foundation for this abstinence, as the injurious effect of grape-sugar upon the decaying teeth is well-known. But all of heathen superstitions cannot be so happily explained. One god would impose upon me abstinence from the use of eggs, another from beans, till after I made all my vows, many of my boyish delicacies were entered upon the prohibition list. Multiplicity of gods often involved the contradiction of the requirements of one god with those of another, and sad was the plight of a conscientious soul when he had to satisfy more than one god. With so many gods to satisfy and appease, I was naturally a fretful timid child. I framed a general prayer to be offered to every one of them, adding of course special requests appropriate to each, as I happened to pass before each temple. Every morning as soon as I washed myself, I offered this common prayer to each of the four groups of gods located in the four points of the compass, paying special attention to the eastern group, as the Rising Sun was the greatest of all gods. Where several temples were contiguous to one another, the trouble of repeating the same prayer so many times was very great; and I would often prefer a longer route with less number of sanctuaries in order to avoid the trouble of saying my prayers without scruples of my conscience.

The number of dieties to be worshipped increased day by day, till I found my little soul totally incapable of pleasing them all. But a relief came at last

CHAPTER II.

INTRODUCTION TO CHRISTIANITY.

One Sunday morning a school-mate of mine asked me whether I would not go with him to "a certain place in foreigners' quarter, where we can hear pretty women sing, and a tall big man with long beard shout and howl upon an elevated place, flinging his arms and twisting his body in all fantastic manners, to all which admittance is entirely free." Such was his description of a Christian house of worship conducted in the language which was new to me then. I followed my friend, and I was not displeased with the place. Sunday after Sunday I resorted to this place, not knowing the awful consequence that was to follow such a practice. An old English lady from whom I learned my first lessons in English took a great delight in my church-going, unaware of the fact that sight-seeing, and not truth-seeking, was the only view I had in my "Sunday excursion to the settlement" as I called it.

Christianity was an enjoyable thing to me so long as I was not asked to accept it. Its music, its stories, the kindness shown me by its followers, pleased me immensely. But five years after, when it was formally presented to me to accept, with certain stringent laws to keep and much sacrifice to make, my whole nature revolted against submitting myself to such a course. That I must set aside one day out of seven specially for religious purpose, wherein I must keep myself from all my

other studies and enjoyments, was a sacrifice
which I thought next to impossible to make. And
it was not flesh alone which revolted against accepting the new faith. I early learned to honor
my nation above all others, and to worship my
nation's gods and no others. I thought I could
not be forced even by death itself to vow my
allegiance to any other gods than my country's.
I should be a traitor to my country, and an
apostate from my national faith by accepting a
faith which is exotic in its origin. All my noble
ambitions which had been built upon my former
conceptions of duty and patriotism were to be de-
molished by such an overture. I was then a
Freshman in a new Government College, where by
an effort of a New England Christian scientist,
the whole of the upper class (there were but two
classes then in the whole college) had already
been converted to Christianity. The imperious
attitude of the Sophomores toward the "baby
Freshmen" is the same the world over, and when
to it was added a new religious enthusiasm and
spirit of propagandism, their impressions upon
the poor "Freshies" can easily be imagined. They
tried to convert the Freshies by storm; but there
was one among the latter who thought himself
capable of not only withstanding the combined
assault of the "Sophomoric rushes," (in this case,
religion-rush, not cane-rush), but even of recon-
verting them to their old faith. But alas! mighty
men around me were falling and surrendering to
the enemy. I alone was left a "heathen," the much
detested idolator, the incorrigible worshipper of
wood and stones. I well remember the extremity
and loneliness to which I was reduced then. One
afternoon I resorted to a heathen temple in the
vicinity, said to have been "authorized by the

Government" to be the guardian-god of the district. At some distance from the sacred mirror which represented the invisible presence of the deity, I prostrated myself upon coarse dried grass, and there burst into a prayer as sincere and genuine as any I have ever offered to my Christian God since then. I beseeched that guardian-god to speedily extinguish the new enthusiasm in my college, to punish such as those who obstinately refused to disown the strange god, and to help me in my humble endeavor in the patriotic cause I was upholding then. After the devotion I returned to my dormitory, again to be tormented with the most unwelcome persuasion to accept the new faith.

The public opinion of the college was too strong against me, which it was beyond my power to withstand. They forced me to sign the covenant given below, somewhat in a manner of extreme temperance men prevailing upon an incorrigible drunkard to sign a temperance pledge. I finally yielded and signed it. I often asked myself whether I ought to have refrained from submitting myself to such a coercion. I was but a mere lad of sixteen then, and the boys who thus forced me "to come in" were all much bigger than I. So, you see, my first step toward Christianity was a forced one, against my will, and I must confess, somewhat against my conscience too. The covenant I signed read as follows:

COVENANT OF BELIEVERS IN JESUS.

"The undersigned members of S. A. College, desiring to confess Christ according to his command, and to perform with true fidelity every Christian duty in order to show our love and gratitude to that blessed Savior who has made atonement for our sins by his death on the cross; and earnestly wishing to advance his Kingdom among men for the promotion of his glory and the salvation of those for whom he died, do solemnly covenant with God and with each other from this time forth to be his faithful disciples, and to live in strict compliance with the letter and the spirit of his teachings; and whenever a suitable opportunity offers we promise to present ourselves for examination, baptism and admission to some evangelical church.

"We believe the Bible to be the only direct revelation in language from God to man, and the only perfect and infallible guide to a glorious future life.

"We believe in one everlasting God who is our Merciful Father, our just and sovereign Ruler, and who is to be our final Judge.

"We believe that all who sincerely repent and by faith in the Son of God obtain the forgiveness of their sins, will be graciously guided through this life by the Holy Spirit and protected by the watchful providence of the Heavenly Father, and so at length prepared for the enjoyments and pursuits of the redeemed and holy ones; but that all who refuse to accept the invitation of the Gospel must perish in their sins, and be forever punished from the presence of the Lord.

"The following commandments we promise to remember and obey through all the vicissitudes of our earthly lives:

"Thou shalt love the Lord thy God with all thy heart and with all thy soul, and with all thy strength and with all thy mind; and thy neighbor as thyself.

"Thou shalt not worship any graven image or any likeness of any created being or thing.

"Thou shalt not take the name of the Lord thy God in vain.

"Remember the Sabbath day to keep it holy, avoiding all unnecessary labor, and devoting it as far as possible to the study of the Bible and the preparation of thyself and others for a holy life.

"Thou shalt obey and honor thy parents and rulers.

"Thou shalt not commit murder, adultery, or other impurity, theft or deception.

"Thou shalt do no evil to thy neighbor.

"Pray without ceasing.

"For mutual assistance and encouragement we hereby constitute ourselves an association under the name "Believers in Jesus," and we promise faithfullly to attend one or more meetings each week while living together, for the reading of the Bible or other religious books or papers, for conference and for social prayer; and we sincerely desire the manifest presence in our hearts of the Holy Spirit to quicken our love, to strengthen our faith, and to guide us into a saving knowledge of the truth. S.—March 5, 1877."

The whole was framed in English by the American Christian scientist mentioned before, himself a graduate of, and once a professor in, one of the most evangelical of the New England Colleges. His own signature was followed by those of the fifteen of his students, and my class-mates swelled the number to over thirty. My name, I suppose, stood the last but one or two.

The practical advantage of the new faith was evident to me at once. I had felt it even while I was engaging all my powers to repel it from me. I was taught that there was but one God in the

Universe, and not many,—over eight millions,—
as I had formerly believed. The Christian monotheism laid its axe at the root of all my superstitions. All the vows I had made, and the manifold
forms of worship with which I had been attempting to appease my angry gods, could now be dispensed with by owning this one God; and my
reason and conscience responded "yea!" One
God, and not many, was indeed a glad tiding to
my little soul. No more use of saying my long
prayers every morning to the four groups of gods
situated in the four points of the compass; of
repeating a long prayer to every temple I passed
by in the streets; and of observing this day for
this god and that day for that god, with vows and
abstinence peculiar to each. (Oh, how proudly I
passed by temples after temples with my head
erect and conscience clear, with full confidence
that they could punish me no longer for my not
saying my prayers to them, for I found the God of
gods to back and uphold me.) My friends noticed
the change in my mood at once. While I used to
stop my conversation as soon as a temple came in
view, for I had to say my prayer to it in my heart,
they observed me to continue in cheer and laughter all through my way to the school. I was not
sorry that I was forced to sign the covenant of the
"Believers in Jesus." Monotheism made me a new
man. I resumed my beans and eggs. I thought
I comprehended the whole of Christianity, so inspiring was the idea of one God. The new spiritual freedom given by the new faith had a healthy
influence upon my mind and body. My studies
were pursued with more concentration. Rejoicing in the newly-imparted activity of my body I
roamed over fields and mountains, observed the
lillies of the valley and birds of the air, and sought

to commune through Nature with Nature's God. A few extracts from my Diary may now be inserted.

Sept. 9, 1877—Took walk with S. and M. in morning. In evening heard the Christ-prayer of the Sophomores.

"Christ-prayer," a peculiar expression, this. I discern a sort of scorn in it.

Dec. 1.—Entered the gate of the "Jesus Religion."

Or rather forced to enter; i. e. forced to sign the covenant of the "Believers in Jesus."

Feb. 10, 1878, Sunday.—O., a Sophomore, comes and talks in my room (about Christianity). Took walk with T., M., F., H., and Ot., by the river. On the way home observed the killing of street dogs. In evening, O. comes again, and played "lots" with us.

Not very puritanic way of keeping Sabbath. O. turned out to be the pastor of our church in after years. We called him a "missionary monk," and he was the one who teased me most while I was yet a heathen. The extermination of houseless dogs was going on then, and the boys liked to witness the cruel process, and we thought it was not a sin to do so even on Sundays. "Lots" was our favorite play in which good and bad lucks were distributed in chance manners among the players; and our would-be pastor and clergyman thought it was not below his sacerdotal dignity to join such a party in Sunday evening.

March 3, Sunday.—Had a tea-party in afternoon. A church in O.'s room in evening.

Pleasures of flesh still indulged in on holy days. O. is still the centre of the religious movement, and a "church," or more properly a religious meeting, was held for the first time in his room.

March 31, Sunday.—A church in Ot.'s room. The chapter of the evening was really interesting.

I think the chapter was Romans XII. Our conscience was pricked, because we were not in mood "to feed our enemy in his hunger."

April 21, Sunday.—At 9 in morning had a prayer meeting with F., M., Ot., H., and T. Great joy for the first time.

Getting to be more spiritual. Began to feel joy in prayers.

May 19, Sunday.—Too much criticism in the meeting. In afternoon, rambled in the forest with F., Ot., M., A., and T. Brought some cherry-blossoms with us. Very pleasant.

A germ of religious dissension already, which was dissipated by flower-hunting in the spring air. The best way of settling difficulties in any church, I suppose.

June 1, Saturday.—The day for the College sport. No recitations. Some two hundred spectators on the ground. Regular

stomach-stuffing in the hall in evening. A
scuffle with H.

Very unfitting preparation for the day that
followed. H. was a "church" member, and I dis-
agreed with him on some theological opinions.

June 2, Sunday.—At 10 A. M. heard a
sermon from Rev. Mr. H. At 3 P. M. after
another sermon and prayers, received baptism from him, together with the six brothers
Ot., M., A., H., T., and F. Prayer and sermon
in evening once more.

A never-to-be-forgotten day. Mr. H. was a
Methodist missionary from America, who came
once a year to render us help in religious matters.
We remember how we kneeled before him, and
how tremblingly though resolutely we responded
Amen, as we were asked to own the name of Him
who was crucified for our sins. We thought that
each of us should adopt a Christian name at the
same time as we confessed ourselves as Christians
before men. So we looked over the appendix to
Webster's dictionary, and each selected a name
as it seemed well fitted to him. Ot. called himself
Paul: he was literary in his inclination, and he
thought the name of a pupil of Gamaliel would
go very well with him. F. adopted Hugh for his
Christian name for no other reason than that it
sounded very much like his nick-name "Nu" meaning "bald-headed." T. was called Frederick, A.,
Edwin, H., Charles, M., Francis, and I named
myself Jonathan, because I was a strong advocate
of the virtue of friendship, and Jonathan's love
for David pleased me well.

The Rubicon was thus crossed forever. We vowed our allegiance to our new Master, and the sign of the Cross was made upon our brows. Let us serve Him with the loyalty we have been taught to show toward our earthly lord and master, and go on conquering kingdom after kingdom,

"Till earth's remotest nation
Has learned Messiah's name."

Once we were converted, we too became missionaries. But a church must first be organized.

CHAPTER III.

THE INCIPIENT CHURCH.

Now that we were baptized we felt we were new men; at least we tried to feel so, and to appear so. Within a month we were to give up the humiliating name of the "Freshies," and with the advent of younger brothers below us, we thought we ought to behave more like men and less like children. Christians and Sophomores ought to be exemplars in conduct and scholarship to heathens and Freshmen. But heathenism and Freshmanism were not to be given up without due farewells to them. At the close of the term, therefore, the converted Freshmen assembled together,—it was not on a Sunday though,—and repeated on a grander scale than ever before a *fete* of the two *isms* we were leaving behind us. Edwin was sent to the farm to procure the biggest squash he could find, together with a quantity of radishes, cabbages and tomatoes. Francis our Botanist knew where the dandalion leaves could be found, and I was sent with his tin-can to pick up the can-full of these delicious plants. Frederick who was a skilled Chemist and always foremost in both the theory and practice of the Culinary Science, was ready with his alkali, salts, and sugar; and Hugh contributed his proficiency in Mathematics and Physics by kindling the hottest fire for our purpose. The literary Paul was always lazy at such a time, though he was second to none when the consumption began. When all was ready, a signal was given for the consumption, and the whole was dispatched in half an hour. Since then we tried to care less about our stomachs, and more about our souls.

Before entering into the description of the little "church" we formed in our private rooms, I must notice here some of the personal traits of its members.

The eldest of us was Hugh. He was a Mathematician and Engineer; was always practical, and had solid cash in view, of course with Christian aim. He need not inquire much into the reasons of Christianity, provided it could make men fair and square in business. He hated meanness and hypocrisy of all sorts, and his tact in tricks, of which he had a fertile resource, often cropped out in the "church," inflicting peculiarly painful wounds upon his victims. He has ever been a reliable financial supporter of the church, has often been its treasurer, and calculated "strength of materials" for our new church-building some years afterward.

Next in age came Edwin. He was a good-hearted fellow, foremost in everything, ready with his tears when his sympathy was called for, and was always serviceable as "Commissioner for Arrangement." At Christmas, in Dedication services, he would often "forget his meals" to have all things look nice and pretty. Dig in theology was not his. Some stories from the illustrated religious papers impressed him more and drew more of his abundant tears than the best argument in "Butler's Analogy" or "Liddon's Bampton Lectures."

Francis had the roundest character among us, with "malice toward none, and charity toward all." "He is naturally good," we used to say, "and

he need not exert himself to be good." His
presence was peace, and when the incipient church
was on the point of dissolution on account of
personal animosities or *odium theologicum* among
its members, he was the cynosure around which
we began to revolve once more in peace and harmony. He turned to be the best Botanist in the
country, and as a Christian layman his service
has always been invaluable in the advancement
of God's kingdom among his countrymen.

Frederick, like Hugh, was a practical man, but
with shrewdness and insight uncommon with a
boy of his age. His favorite study was Chemistry,
and he became one of the foremost Technologists
in the country. His literary accomplishment was
considerable. He mastered German and French
without the help of instructors and could enjoy
Schiller, Milton and Shakespeare. He doubted
some of the fundamental teachings of Christianity, but he early saw the impossibility
of disposing of all such difficulties by applying
himself at them. He pressed on with a "pure,
spotless life" in view, and as far as human judgement goes, he attained it. His too-much practical
common-sense was sometimes not very congenial
with the boyish air of the "church." Still he bore,
and we bore, and for four long years, he very
seldom was absent from the meeting.

Paul was a "scholar." He often suffered from
neuralgia, and was near-sighted. He could doubt
all things, could manufacture new doubts, and
must test and prove everything before he could
accept it. Thomas he should have surnamed himself. But with his spectacles and all his assumed
scholarly airs, he was a guileless boy at heart;
and he could join with his comrades in a *fete
champetre* under cherry-blossoms in a Sabbath

afternoon, after that very morning having cooled
the enthusiasm of the "church" with his gloomy
and intricate doubts about Providence and Predestination.

Charles was a compound character. He was
second only to Frederick in his shrewd common
sense, but was more like Paul in his intellectual
attitude toward Christianity. He like many
other ardent youths tried to comprehend God and
Universe by the aid of his intellect, and to conform himself to the very letter of God's eternal
law by his own efforts; in which failing, he oscil-
lated to an entirely different aspect of Christianity, and settled in his faith in the "gospel of good
works." He turned to be a learned engineer, and
his sympathy in substantial forms can always be
relied upon when some practical good is con-
templated either within or without the church.

Jonathan need not confess himself, as he is the
subject of our study in this little volume.

Such were "the seven" that formed the little
"church." With us joined for the first two years
one S., "Kahau" we nicknamed him, for he appeared as stub and acute as that monkey tribe.
He was baptized a year before us, and had more
of Christian experience than any one of "the
seven."

The Juniors had their religious meetings by
themselves, and we, the Christian Sophomores,
assembled by ourselves, but in the Sunday evening both joined together for the study of the
Bible. It was generally acceded, however, that
the Sophomores were more earnest than the
Juniors, and our meeting was often coveted by
the more earnest among the latter.

Our Sunday services were conducted on this
wise: The little church was entirely democratic,

and every one of us stood on the same ecclesiastical footing as the rest of the members. This we found to be thoroughly Biblical and Apostolic. The leadership of the meeting therefore devolved upon each one of us in turn. He was to be our pastor, priest, and teacher,—even servant,—for the day. He was responsible for calling us together at the appointed time, his room was to be our church, and he must look how we were to be seated there. He alone could sit upon a stool, and his people sat before him in the true oriental fashion, upon blankets spread upon the floor. For our pulpit the mechanical Hugh fitted up a flour-barrel which we covered with a blue blanket. Thus dignified, the pastor opened the service with a prayer, which was followed by reading from the Bible. He then gave a little talk of his own, and called up each of his sheep to give a talk of *his* own in turn. Sometime after we were baptized, Paul made a motion that some eatables be introduced to our meetings to serve as "attractions," to which we all agreed. Therefore, the first thing on a Sunday morning was for the pastor of the day to make collections for this purpose, and to provide for the meeting some sweet things. Frederick favored the quality, but Hugh and Charles urged upon the quantity of these "attractions," but we left the selection to the choice of the pastor. Thus provided, with water and tea besides, the service began; and when the pastor finished his talk, his helper distributed the cakes equally among the members; and "talks" went on as we helped ourselves with these refreshments. Each one made his own characteristic talk. Hugh's favorite book was "Nelson on Infidelity," and he condemned unbelief with his usual hatred against unfaithfulness of all sorts.

Edwin would tell how Susie and Charlie saw the goodness of God in "snow, beautiful snow," and how the merciful Providence fed helpless little birdies with tender grubs. Frederick's talks were usually short. His usual subject was the majesty of God, and awe and reverence we should pay to Him. Charles would read a page or so from Liddon's "Bampton Lectures" which he specially ordered from England, but he could only half-understand what was stated therein, and we his hearers even less. Paul's talks were essentially argumentative, and were always scholarly and well prepared. Francis never failed to inculcate upon us something solid and thoughtful. Jonathan would pour out his heart before them, whether it be fear or joy that engrossed him at the moment. "Kahau" read a chapter from the "Village Sermons" which we always enjoyed, but his talks were often altogether too long. Our sweet-meats were consumed usually long before the talks were over, and the rest of the time we kept our mouths moving by the occasional draughts of our unsugared and unmilked tea. The dinner-bell at half-past 12 o'clock was the signal for the close of the meeting. The apostolic benediction was said, and on we hastened to the dining room, after some four hours' continual sitting upon the hard floor.

As no religious books in our vernacular were available for our purpose, we had recourse mostly to English and American publications. By the effort of some of our Christian friends, some eighty volumes of the publications of the American Tract Society were secured, and the bound volumes of the "Illustrated Christian Weeklies" were endless sources of enjoyments to us. We had also about one hundred volumes sent by the London Tract Society and the Soc. of Promoting Christian Knowledge. Later, the Unitarian Association of Boston kindly contributed to us a good set of their publications, which too we were not afraid to read. But the books that helped us most were the well-known Commentaries by the lamented Rev. Albert Barnes of Philadelphia. The deep spirituality that pervades these volumes their simple but lucid style and so much of Puritanism in them as to serve as healthy astringents upon the young converts in a heathen land, made these commentaries specially useful and fascinating to us. I believe by the end of my college course I read every word in his commentaries upon the New Testament, and the theological stamp of this worthy divine has never been removed from my mind. Blessed is he that makes good books!

Our week-day prayer-meeting was held on the Wednesday evening at half-past 9 o'clock. There were no "talks," but all prayed, and it took an hour for the meeting to close. An hour's continual kneeling upon the hard floor was not very comfortable. We learned afterward from our professor in physiology that such a prolonged kneeling, if long continued, might result in synovitis of the knee-joints.

We took comparatively little part in the united Bible-meeting in Sunday evening with the members of the upper class. There O. the "Missionary Monk," S. the "Eldest," and W. the "Crocodile" had more ponderous arguments than we could offer for the defence and vindication of Christianity. We were usually glad when this meeting was over, when we had our own private service to refresh us once more before we closed this most enjoyable day of the week.

With these remarks I am ready to give some more of extracts from my diaries.

June 19, ~~1877.~~ *1878.*—Went to the theater with the "six brothers."

Not three weeks yet after we were baptized!

July 5.—Received $17.50 as prizes for excellency in my studies. In afternoon, went to theatre with the whole class.

We early disassociated theater-going from Christianity. I did not go with very clear conscience, this for the second time since I was baptized. But this was the last for me in my life thus far to cross the threshold of a theater of any description. I have learned, however, in after years that Christians may go to theater without detriment to the welfare of their souls, and that many of them really *do* go. Yes, theater-going may not be a sin as adultery is sin, but if I can get along without these "amusements that kill," I believe I can just as well stay away from them without much detriment to my body or mind.

Sept. 29, Sunday.—Spent the afternoon in the forest with the "six brothers." Enjoyed wild grapes and berries, prayed and sang. Very fine day.

One of those never-to-be-forgotten days when we uplifted our hearts to our Creator in the primeval forest.

Oct. 20, Sunday.—Climbed the "Stone-Hill" with the "seven brothers." Prayed and sang as usual. Refreshed with the wild berries on the way back.

Another such day. We were not permitted to sing in our rooms, neither had we courage to do so, as we sang each in his own way, and there was no "musical melody" in our voices uncultivated and tunes untutored. Paul said he could sing all hymns with "Toplady," which was really the only tune he knew! Yet, hills and mountains could bear with our music, and God knows that our songs had one element of good music in them—the feeling heart.

Dec. 1.—Joined the Methodist Episcopal Church through Mr. H.

The Rev. Mr. H. our beloved missionary was again in the town, and we joined his church without scrutinizing pro or con of his or any other denomination. We only knew he was a good man, and thought that his church must be good too.

Dec. 8, Sunday.—In evening, had serious talks with the "seven brothers." We confessed our inmost thoughts to each other, and promised to bring about great reformations in our hearts.

The best day we had had since we accepted Christianity. I believe we talked and prayed until long after midnight, for it was not many hours before the day dawned after we went to our beds. Everybody appeared like an angel on that night. The "spiny" Jonathan, the "knobby" Hugh, and the "scraggy" Frederick were as round as the "globular" Francis on that evening.

The skeptic Paul found no objections against such a Christianity. O for more of such a night like this! Was that night more beautiful than this, when the angelic choir was heard in the heaven, and the Star of Bethlehem led the wise men of the East to the Infant Jesus!

Dec. 25, Christmas.—Commemorated the coming to the earth of our Savior. No end to our pleasures.

The first Christmas we have had. The Juniors had "no faith" for this celebration. They imitated us the next year.

Dec. 29, Sunday.—Etc., etc., about the oil in evening.

This was the last Sabbath of the year, and the Christian members of both classes were seriously considering all the faults and short-comings of the year that was closing, and all the hopes and possibilities of the year that was coming. Our prayers and exhortations were unusually earnest that evening. But all at once we heard some one crying that Prof. I. was back, and that he would demonstrate to us the possibility of making as good light with the rape-seed oil as with the kerosene. The fact was that the government authority passed a decree some weeks ago that imported articles be dispensed with as much as possible, and the kerosene oil coming all from the hills of Pennsylvania and New York must be substituted by the rape-seed oil of our own production. Our Yankee lamps therefore were all confiscated, and new lamps to burn the vegetable oil were offered us. But the light so made was miserably poor compared with the light given by the American mineral oil, and this served as a good excuse for neglect in our study. Mr. I. was an instructor in Mathematics, and we did not like him much. That Sunday night he was well saturated with alcohol, and his locomotory and vocal organs were not entirely under his control. To the usual complaints of one of the students about the new lamps, he replied that a little more common sense on our part would prove the case to be otherwise, and he was going to demonstrate to us his statement in a scientific manner. The opportunity was a good one to demonstrate to him how much we regarded him. Both Christians and non-Christians united in this demonstration. Some of our semi-heathen Junior brothers, such as Y. the "Square-faced," U. the "Good-natured," and T. the "Pterodactyl" threw their Bibles upon the floor, and rushed at once into the scene of excitement. The professor's scientific demonstration was not what he wanted. We took him outside, rolled him in snow, aimed at him a good number of snow-balls, and called him by all kinds of ungentlemanly names. Our Charles who was then in his best religious mood entreated us to withhold ourselves from such unchristian acts, but all in vain. After the poor professor under the influence of the alcoholic stimulus was well tempered in the snow, the boys returned to the sacred meeting, and there was no St. Ambrose to keep out these little Theodosii from the room of worship. The sensation we experienced that Sunday evening can never be forgotten. Few penitential prayers were said, and the meeting was adjourned till the next year. Every one of us felt that Christ was not present in that meeting; or if he was, He left it as soon as some of us rushed out of the room to attack our poor professor with snow-balls. How far our practical Christianity was lagging behind our theoretic Christianity, we sincerely felt that evening.

March 9, 1879.—A change in the way of conducting our prayer-meetings.

We were afraid of "synovitis" by too much continued kneeling. The general cry was for short prayers. The same things were not to be repeated in one and the same meeting. This curtailed the service to about 20 minutes, and we were not a little relieved.

I think it was about this time when an episode occurred in our usual prayer-meeting, which I failed to note down in my diary. The day was a Wednesday, and we were quite tired down after three hours' manual labour upon the college farm. After heavy meals and usual drudging over our lessons, we were not in very fine mood to engage in spiritual communion with a Higher Power. But the rule was not to be changed, and when the bell rang Frederick who was our pastor for the evening gathered his sheep together for prayer. He kneeled by the flour-barrel, his head imbedded in his folded arms upon the pulpit, and opened the meeting with his short prayer. The other boys followed him one by one, each wishing that the meeting be closed as soon as possible. We were glad when the last one prayed, and were impatient to be excused at once by our pastor when the last amen was said. It was said and responded to, but the pastor was silent. His apostolic benediction did not come, and nobody else had the authority to adjourn the meeting. There was a perfect silence for about five minutes,—a long time for that night. We could kneel no longer. Jonathan was kneeling beside the pastor. He lifted up his head to see what was the matter with Frederick. Behold the pastor was fast asleep upon the flour-barrel, and no wonder no benediction came! We might sit up the whole night if we waited for his holy words. Jonathan thought the case was exceptional, and that the rule could be temporarily modified on such an occasion without the consent of our "ecumenical council." So he rose, and said in a solemn voice: "As our brother Frederick fell asleep, God will pardon me to exercise the pastor's office. May the grace of our Lord Jesus Christ, etc. Amen." "Amen" all responded, and up came our tired heads. But Frederick's was upon the barrel, as immovable as a log. Charles shook him, and he awoke. He was going to dismiss us with his benediction,—he did not forget his duty in the dreamland,—but it was already said, and we were ready to separate. It was too bad for Frederick that he slept on his pulpit, but we could all forgive him, for we were all very sleepy on that night. Even the holy Apostles slept while their Master was praying, and why not we young Christians after hard labor and good square meals!

May 11, Sunday.—Cherry-blossom hunting in afternoon.

May 18, Sunday.—Excursion to the forest in afternoon.

June 2, Monday.—The anniversary of our new birth (that is, of baptism). Tea-party with the seven brothers, and pleasant conversations for several hours.

The commemoration of our spiritual birth-day. I see no reason why we should not remember this day, and have as nice time as on the day our mothers gave us birth to this weary earth. Yet with many a Christian both in my country and others, the spiritual birth-day seems to have not half as many kind words and beautiful presents as the day of the advent of our perishable body to this earth.

June 15, Sunday.—The day of festival for the guardian god of the district. Very much distressed. But I did see horse-race, I did accept invitation from Francis' uncle (for "cardinal pleasures") and I did gormandize. Alas!

Our puritanic Sabbath was much disturbed by the heathen festival, and I yielded to the temptations. "Though I would do good, evil was present with me; and with the flesh I served the law of sin. O wretched man that I was!"

The summer of 1879 I spent in my home in the metropolis, some 600 miles south of where my college was, the good Francis accompanying me in the travel. The chief aim I had in taking this long journey was to preach the gospel of Christ to my father and mother, brothers and sisters. It was very pleasant to come home after two years' absence from it. Wherever there was a mission station on our way, we called upon our Christian friends, and religion was the main topic of our conversations. I told my mother that I became a new man in S., and that she too must become what I became. But she was so much taken up with the joy of seeing her son again that she cared nothing about what I told her about Christianity. Usual oblations were offered to the family idols to return thanks for my safe arrival, which of course gave me sore pain in my heart. I often retired to my closet to beseech my Savior to save this heathen home. I did sincerely believe that unbaptized souls were in the danger of eternal condemnation in the hell, and my whole energy was directed toward the conversion of my family members. But the mother was indifferent, the father was decidedly antagonistic, and my younger brother who afterward became a fine Christian was so provoking as to have turned a copy of the Epistle to the Romans which I gave him into a "codex rescriptus," writing in between the sacred columns something to show his contempt of Christianity. Yet I persevered and continued on praying, till near the time of my departure for my college I succeeded in extracting from my father a promise to examine the faith I implored him to receive.

While in the metropolis, I met with many "brothers and sisters," and feasted upon sermons and addresses which it was wholly impossible to hear in the place where my college was. I believed that Christians were an entirely different set of people from heathens, and that the fellow-disciples of Christ ought to stick closer than brothers to each other. We knew such was the case among the brethren in our little church, and thought the same was true throughout the church universal. So confident, so unsuspicious, we were received with welcome everywhere, and we thought our beliefs on that point were correct. We saw several good churches, with pulpits, not

like ours made of a flour-barrel, rows of benches
far superior to our blue-blankets spread upon the
hard floor, organs to attune voices, etc.   They all
made us eagerly anticipate the time, when after
finishing our college-course we would have a
church made for us like those we saw in the more
civilized part of our country.   There also we were
taught in many things, and among the rest, how to
say our grace before our meals.   This we never
had done thus far, and we went at once to our
meals, as dogs and heathens do when they are
hungry.   We paid a visit to a native Methodist
minister, and there was also present with him one
Mr. Y., a young Presbyterian.   They asked us to
stop for the dinner, which we gladly did; and
when a little wooden stand with a cupfull of white
rice, a fish, and some vegetables upon it was placed
before each of us, Francis and I in our usual savage style, lifted our chop-sticks, and proceeded
right at once to help ourselves.   Mr. Y. then
gravely said, "Do you not pray before you eat?
Let us pray."   We stood abashed, laid our sticks
down, bowed our heads as they did, and waited
for the outcome.   The grace was said, but we
hesitated to commence eating, for we were afraid
we might be asked to do something more.   They
then kindly told us to begin.   I still remember
every word that was said then, and everything
that was offered me to eat.   The fish was a gray
sole, with five black horizontal bars across its
back, its mouth on the left side of the body and
making a curvature a little above the pectoral fin.
I did observe all this while I cast down my eyes
in shame and confusion.   But the lesson once
taught has never been forgotten since.   We
taught it to our brethren when we returned to
our college in the Fall, and the "grace-less" meals

soon became signs of the reprobate among us. On many an occasion in after years, where religion was held in scorn and contempt, and prayers before meals were watched with ridicule, I have never failed to stick to the practice I learned in a Methodist minister's room.

Aug. 25, Monday.—Reached S. at 7 P. M. No end to the joys of the brethren to see us again. Deeply impressed with their love and faithfulness.

Glad to be in our College-home once more. We found a table well spread with tea and sweet things waiting us. We told the brethren all what we saw in the metropolis, mostly about churches and Christians there. The impressions of the metropolitan churches upon us were not altogether satisfactory. We might just as well remain contented with the flour-barrel pulpit and all the rustic simplicities of our own little "church."

Aug. 31, Sunday.—Meeting very interesting.

It could not be otherwise after the absence of two of its members for about two months.

Nothing worth noting down to the end of the year. There was one experiment, however, which we tried in our Sunday services, which must have taken place sometime between this and Christmas. We got tired with our "talks," and some changes in the methods of conducting our meetings were very desirable. One of us made a suggestion that we might prepare ourselves during our College days to meet infidels whom we would be sure to meet when we went into the world. We all discussed the plan, and concluded that the

best methôd would be to divide the "church" into
two divisions, one representing the Christian and
the other the infidel side, and to let each division
take the two sides alternately. The members of
the infidel side were to ask all manner of questions which infidels might ask, and those of the
Christian side were to answer them. The plan
was agreed upon, and it was to be carried into
practice from the next Sunday.

On that day,—the first Sabbath when the meeting was conducted on the new method,—we divided the members into two parties by lots, Charles,
Jonathan, Frederick and Edwin falling into the
Christian side, and Francis, Hugh, Paul and
"Kahau" into the skeptic or infidel side. A War-
burton, a Chalmers, a Liddon and a Gladstone
were arrayed on one side, and a Bolinbroke, a
Hume, a Gibbon and a Huxley on the other.
After prayers and distribution of eatables as
usual, the engagement began. The subject of the
day was the "Existence of God." Francis the first
skeptic attacked Charles the first apologist. To
the challenge that the Universe could have existed
by itself, Charles brought forth arguments showing that matter had unmistakable characteristics
of manufactured articles (the argument borrowed
from Maxwell, I suppose), and that as such it
could not be self-existing. The first attack was
repulsed, and our faith was nobly defended. The
practical Hugh had not many formidable arguments to array against Christianity, and Jonathan's task was not a difficult one to meet his
objections. Now it was conclusively proved that
this Universe *must* have had its Creator, that this
Creator was self-existing, and that He was Almighty and All-wise. But now it was Paul's turn
to make an assault, and Frederick was to meet

him. They had not been on very friendly terms for some days, and we were afraid of the outcome of such an encounter. We have already seen that the scholarly Paul had more doubts than he could answer; and the present occasion gave him the first-rate opportunity to pour out the stiffest doubt he could manufacture in his neuralgic head. "I grant," he began, "that this Universe is a created Universe, that God is All-wise and Almighty, and that nothing is impossible with this God. But how can you prove to me that this God, after He created this Universe and set it in motion so that it can grow and develop by itself with the potential energy imparted by Him,—that this Creator hath not put an end to His own existence and annihilated Himself. If He can do *all* things, why cannot He commit suicide!" An intricate, almost blasphemous question! How can the practical Frederick dispose of this question? Our eyes were fixed upon the perplexed apologist, and even the infidel side was solicitous about Fred's answer. For a moment he was silent, but the triumphant Paul still pressed on with his attack. Frederick must say something. Mustering his courage, he said in a scornful way, "Well, only fools will ask such questions." "Why, fools? you call me a fool then?" retorted the exasperated Paul. "Yes, I should say so," was Frederick's determined answer. Paul could hold himself no longer. "Brethren," he said, as he rose and beat his breast, "I can bear this company no longer." Away he rushed out of the room, the door violently shut after him, and we heard him groaning till he reached his own room. The rest of us were taken up with dismay. Some said Paul was wrong, others that Frederick was wrong too. The important question in issue was laid aside. We were now anxious how to reconcile the belligerent parties. The meeting was closed without further discussions, and the new plan was given up altogether. We found out 'that we ourselves had more doubts than we could answer, and that perhaps the best way would be for us to solve them in our own hearts with the help from on high. The next Sunday we resumed our old method, and the lion and the ox did lie together in peace.

Dec. 24, Christmas Eve.—Examination in surveying. Busy with Edwin in arranging for the evening. The meeting began at 7 P. M. All the Christians were present as one body. Eatings and tea-drinkings and miscellaneous talks till 11 P. M. No end to our pleasures.

Our upper-class men united with us in the Christmas feast this year. The commemoration was made on a grander scale than it was the last year. The college kindly lent us a recitation hall which we nicely decorated, and enough contributions were made to make the festival truly enjoyable. There was wrestling of a white and red "Darumas,"* the latter very ingeniously fitted up by one John K., an upper-class man. Y. the "Square-Faced" rolled himself into the effigy, and when it first appeared everybody thought it was nothing but a common idol, "with eyes that see not, and ears that cannot understand." All at once, however, its eyes began to move, the "apodal Daruma" stood upon its own feet, two arms were

* Dharma,—a Chinese Buddhist. whose images are common toys for children. He is usually represented as having no feet.

thrust forth through his sides, and the whole began to dance. Then a white Daruma came out to meet him, and the two wrestled under the umpireship of Jonathan. O, it was such fun! When they retired, there came out a savage, naked except round his loin, and the same was no other than S. the "Eldest," who as the tallest and oldest boy among the Christians, was always looked upon as our leader in religious matters. He danced in this formidable attire, and retired. We did laugh till our diaphrams were well nigh gone down. We were so glad that our Savior came down to the earth to save us. Four hundred years ago, Savonarola instituted such holy carnivals in Florence, and the monks danced as they sang.

> "Never was there so sweet a gladness,
> Joy of so pure and strong a fashion,
> As with zeal, love, and passion,
> Thus to embrace Christ's holy madness.
> Cry with me, cry now as I cry,
> Madness, madness, holy madness!"

Dec. 25.—Meeting at half-past 10 o'clock. The greatest pleasures (holy) since we came to S.

This was a true thanksgiving meeting. No tea or cakes in this meeting. There were prayers and serious talks, S. the "Eldest" leading the meeting. O. the "Missionary Monk" gave us a talk on the history and *raison d'etre* of the Christmas festival. Indeed everybody was serious that morning. I heard in New Orleans that Lent with its fastings and penance is preceded by carnivals

of the wildest sort. Only we were not so in-
dulgent as the Louisianians.

Nothing further is noted down till

**March 28, 1880, Sunday.—Meeting greatly
declines in interest.**

We could not hold ourselves in white heat all
the while. Indeed, there was a decided flagging
in our enthusiasm all through the spring of this
year. Sometimes some petty affairs among the
members disturbed the peace and harmony of the
whole "church." Once we prayed with our faces
turned toward the walls, saying something "insinuating" in our prayers, not to be heard, of course,
by our Father in Heaven, but by the one these
words were aimed at. Yet with all these, we for-
sook not "the assembling of ourselves together."
Heb. X, 25.

June was a busy month to us religiously. We
celebrated our second anniversary of our new
birth with the usual hilarity. The snow having
melted and the fair weather setting in, we had
visits from three missionaries in succession,—one
American and two British,—and our hungry souls
were fed with good supplies of sermons and other
religious instructions. The Hon. Mr. U., a British
consul in a neighboring sea-port, was also here,
and in the house where he stayed, there was held
an Episcopal service on the grandest scale we
ever had witnessed so far. The general impression of the service upon the boys was that it was
somewhat "Buddhistic," its liturgy and surplice
being not entirely consonant with our idea of
simplicity in religion. The notable event in this
service was the demeanor of our semi-heathenish
U. the "Good-Natured," T. the "Pterodactyl," and

some others, who burst into a loud laughter when
they saw two English ladies saluting each other
by bringing their lips in contact. We read in the
Bible how Laban kissed his sons and daughters,
but had never seen the actual kissing before.
Our misdemeanor was really inexcusable.

In July the upper-class graduated, and the
cause of Christianity was much strengthened
thereby. There were eight Christians among
them, viz.: S. the "Eldest," O. the "Missionary
Monk," U. the "Good-Natured," T. the "Pterodactyl," John K. an Episcopalian, W. the "Crocodile," K. the "Patagonian" and Y. the "Square-
Faced." All very nice fellows; and notwithstanding the semi-heathenish appearances of some of
them, and remnants of sinful and tricky propensities inherited from their ancestors, they were
in the bottom of their hearts genuine Christian
gentlemen. We take a photograph together,
dine together, and discuss about the erection of a
house of worship in a near future. Within a
year, we the remaining eight shall join them, and
together we shall carry the Gospel of Christ to the
people among whom we live.

Sept. 18—The Rev. Mr. D. arrives here.

Sept. 19, Sunday.—Made a call upon Mr. D.

Sept. 20.—An English service by Mr. D. in
the evening.

Mr. D. took the place of our beloved missionary Mr. H., and he was now on the second visit
to our place. We had something to tell him
about our plan for the future church, to which
he did not give all his consents.

Oct. 3.—Consultation about the new church building.

Now that several Christians have gone out into the active world, we may have a church of our own; and we are not idle in planning for it.

Oct. 15.—The Revs. Messrs. Den. and P. are here. We meet them at Mr. N.'s.

Have frequent visits from missionaries this year. Messrs. Den. and P. are Episcopalians. Our movements are calling forth the attention of the religious world, and we are not neglected.

Oct. 17, Sunday.—Meeting at Mr. S.'s. Six baptisms. Holy Sacrament at 3 P. M.

Numbers are being added to our holy company, thank God. One thing we were sorry about; i. e. there were distinct tendencies toward our having two churches in the little place, one an Episcopalian, and the other a Methodist church. "One Lord, one faith, one baptism," we began to ponder in our hearts. What is the use of having two separate Christian communities, when even one is not strong enough to stand upon its own feet. We felt for the first time in our Christian experience the evils of denominationalism.

Nov. 21, Sunday.—All the Christians of the place are in the meeting.

Since our upper-class men graduated, we have not had a full meeting for a long while. Now that we meet all together, we discuss once more about the new church,—its scope, its constitution, the advisability of having but one church in the place, etc.

Dec. 26, Sunday.—Perplexed about "Election."

Our little church discusses once more about the doctrine of Election. The chapter of the morning was Rom. IX.

In the old Bible which I spoiled pretty thoroughly with underscorings and marginal-notings with inks of diverse colors, I find a large interrogation mark (?) hanging like a large fish-hook over the awful and mysterious chapter. Our Paul's pessimistic conclusion was this: "If God made one vessel unto honour and another unto dishonour, there is no use of attempting to be saved, for God will take care of His own, and we shall be saved or damned notwithstanding all our efforts to be otherwise." A similar doubt torments every ruminating Christian in every clime. Well let it be by, for we cannot afford to give up the Bible and Christianity because we cannot comprehend the doctrine of Election.

Jan. 3, 1881.—Invitation from "Palmyra." Games and lots till 9 in the evening.

Our Christian baccalaureates had their home, several of them domiciling under one roof. As their nest lay in the midst of a large farm, away from the habitations of human kind, we called it by the name of the city of the beautiful Zenobia, "the city in the Desert." Such invitations were quite frequent, and they did much to knit our hearts together. We had our love-feasts, more substantial than those of the followers of Wesley, in that ours consisted of beef, pork, chicken, onion, beet, potatoes, all thrown into one iron pot and boiled therein. The Christians, both men and women, surrounded the metallic receptacle and feasted therefrom. Not much of etiquette in this, of course; but oftentimes severity in etiquette is inversely proportional as the square of distance between the communing hearts. "Men who ate rice out of the same kettle" is our popular saying about the intimacy well nigh approaching the bond of blood-relationship; and we believed and still believe in the necessity of some other bonds of union for those who are to fight and suffer for one and the same cause than the breaking of bread and drinking of wine by the hand of an officiating minister. Could such a band be divided into "two churches" even though ministers of two denominations wrote the sign of the Cross upon our foreheads? Yea, we are one, as the chicken we boiled in our kettle was one, and a large potato which Jonathan shared with Hugh after it came out of the stove was one.

Jan. 9, Sunday.—Am appointed one of the Committee for the construction of the new church.

The new church was decided upon, and a committee was appointed therefor. It consisted of S. the "Eldest," W. the "Crocodile," O. the "Missionary Monk," Edwin and myself.

March 18, Friday.—A meeting of the Committee. Decide upon the lot and the building.

We had a letter from Rev. Mr. D. telling us that the Methodist Episcopal Church of America would help us with four hundred dollars to build a new church for us. We did not wish to have it given us; we would only borrow it, to be returned at the earliest possible opportunity. There was a strong reason for having such a desire, which we shall see bye and bye. The lot was to cost one hundred dollars, and the rest we would spend upon the building. But, wait, brethren, four hundred dollars in Mexican silver will be some seven hundred dollars in our paper money; and are you sure you can pay up all this sum within a year or so, each of you receiving, as you do, only thirty dollars for your monthly salary? Uh! Serious! We want, and must have a church, but to be indep......, well we don't know.

March 20, Sunday.—Our carpenter comes and presents us his estimate for the new church building.

The plan of the building looks nice, but we must incur debt for making such a church. Uh!

March 24, Thursday.—Money-order arrives from Mr. D. Have it cashed in the bank. A meeting of the Committee in evening. Write a letter to Mr. D.

The money finally comes. Jonathan is to be the treasurer for a time; and he brings four-inch-thickness of paper money into his room in the college dormitory. It is the largest sum of money he ever has handled in his life. But look, my soul, the money is not thine, neither is it properly the church's. *It is to be returned; use it with caution.*

March 31.—Marriage ceremony of John K. at 7 P. M., Rev. Mr. Den. officiating. Entertainment with tea and cakes afterward. In-

finite pleasures till 10 P. M.   The first marriage among the S. Christians.

John an Episcopalian was the first among the
Christian boys to enter into the state of matri-
monial bliss.   The ceremony was conducted in an
Episcopalian style, the bride and the bridegroom
exchanging their rings at the altar.   It was quite
a departure from the custom we had been used to
in our country.   At the table where refreshments
were served up, several boys made speeches one
after another, and bade success and God-speed
to the new couple.   But we could hardly believe
that he who fitted up a red Dharma for us on a
Christmas eve was now a husband!   "The Lord
make the woman that is come unto thine house
like Rachel and like Leah, which two did build
the house of Isreal."   Ruth IV, 11.   She might in
a similar manner help to build up the house of
God we were planning then.

March 31.—The church matter getting into
troubles.   The Committee meets in evening,
and decides to give up the idea of a new
building.

The fact was, the lot of land which we proposed
to buy was not to be had, and as it was not possible to find another lot, "we must either hang our
church in the air," as K. the "Patagonian" suggested, "after the fashion of Queen Semiramis'
garden, or give up the idea of the new building
altogether."   And we were not sorry that we
came to such a conclusion, for we were extremely
afraid of running into a big debt; and if we could
have any place for worship—be it ever so humble
—we would greatly prefer it to a stately building
built upon our credit.

April 1.—The carpenter is away, and the matter gets into further trouble.

April 3.—S. the "Eldest" talks with the carpenter, and the matter looks to settle fairly.

April 15.—Decide to pay $20 to the carpenter.

The obtrusive Edwin, one of the members of the Committee, made an arrangement with the carpenter to have the timber ready within a fixed period. The carpenter therefore sent his men to mountains to hew the wood. The difficulty was this: Solomon made a verbal contract with Hiram to have a temple built for him in Jerusalem. Hiram believed in Solomon; so he sent his men at once to the Lebanon to cut down its cedars for the royal purpose. But subsequently Solomon found out that the Mt. Moriah where he intended to build his temple was not to be had, for some one else had already possessed it; and he was not very willing to run in debt with Pharaoh, which was necessary in order to execute his plan. So he gave up the plan of building the temple. But the Lebanon was resounding with the axes of the men of Hiram chopping wood for Solomon. Meanwhile Hiram went down to Zidon on his own business account, so that Solomon could not find him out to tell him of the change that was made about the new building. Each day that Solomon delayed in transmitting the news to Hiram involved either party in further troubles; and Solomon and his councillors became uneasy. At last, Hiram returned to Tyre, Solomon informed him that the temple was not to be built, and asked him

to call back all his men from the Lebanon. But
Hiram's men had been in the mountains for over
two weeks, and a considerable number of cedars
and cypresses had been already cut down and prepared for timbers; and Hiram wanted to have the
loss covered by Solomon. Solomon asks his councillors about the matter. S. the "Eldest" and W.
the "Crocodile" read something in Bentham and
John Stuart Mill, and they think that as Solomon
did not put his royal seal upon the contract made
with Hiram, therefore Solomon has no legal obligation to pay for Hiram's loss. But the king's
other councillors, O. the "Missionary Monk" and
Jonathan, think otherwise. Hiram trusted in
Solomon's words as the words of one who believes
in Jehovah and His covenant; and it makes no
difference whether the royal seal was put or not.
The king must pay, or else the house of David
shall lose the confidence of the public. But S.
and W. are strong in their legal convictions, and
the whole people of Israel approve their agree-
ments. O. and Jonathan, however, cannot bear
such a course. They meet one cold winter
morning upon snow, and there come into
the conclusion that they shall bear the
responsibility by themselves. They see Hiram
privately, tell him that they themselves
are poor, but that they are sorry to see him un-
fairly treated. Hiram is touched with the sincerity of the two men of Isreal, says that he too
shall bear a part of the loss, and that $20 from the
Isrealites will satisfy him. Jonathan is yet a
student, and his regular income is only ten cents
a week. O. pays the whole sum, and Jonathan will
settle account with him when the latter will
graduate from the college in the next July. The
whole difficulty was thus settled with little self-

sacrifice on the part of the two of Solomon's councillors. Subsequently, U. the "Good-Natured" and Hugh came to the help of O. and Jonathan, and shared part of the debt the last two incurred.—A petty affair not worth mentioning, my readers may say; but such an experience like this teaches us more about God and man than whole lots of theologies and philosophies we dive into.

April 17, Sunday.—Take walk with Charles in afternoon to seek a house. The Committee meets at the house of S. the "Eldest."

A new building being given up, we begin to find out a house already built.

April 24.—Meet with O., and consult with him about the church.

April 30.—Call upon O. The independence of the church is spoken of for the first time.

We are not very successful in having a house of worship. The members are getting somewhat discouraged. Our Episcopalian brethren have already their house of worship; and why cannot we become one, and all assemble in their church? "Necessity is the mother of inventions." Our failures in having a church drove us to a higher and nobler conception of Christian unity and independence. It was the Spirit that was guiding us!

May 15, Sunday.—The church meets in "Palmyra," and discusses about independence. Opinions are various. The meeting

closed without coming into any definite conclusion.

The matter is getting to be more serious. Let
all the Christians meet, and discuss about this
most important question of the church independence. Jonathan is young, idealistic, and impul-
sive. He sees no difficulty in separating ourselves
from the existing denominations and in consti-
tuting ourselves into a new and independent body.
But S. the "Eldest" and W. the "Crocodile" are
prudent, and they will not have such rashness
committed among us. U. the "Good-Natured" and
O. the "Missionary Monk" take sides with Jonathan, but are not so confident of success as he.
We came to no definite conclusion on that afternoon.

May 22, Sunday.—The church independence is getting to be the public opinion among
its members. Meet with O. in evening, and
draw up a constitution with him.

May 23.—Meet with O., and consult with
him about the church affairs. Entertained
with buck-wheat by him.

The cry for independence is getting upper-hand.
O. and Jonathan attempt a draft of the constitution for the would-be independent church. The
idea that two boys of twenties should undertake
a task which baffled the biggest heads of Europe
and America! Preposterous! But courage! "for
God hath chosen the foolish things of the world
to confound the wise." But let us refresh ourselves with buck-wheat when we get tired.

Near the end of the month, Mr. D. made his

third visit to us, and ministered unto us with sermons, baptisms, and the Lord's supper, as usual. But we could not very well conceal from him our intention of separating ourselves from his church,—the Methodist Episcopal Church,—and he was not very well pleased with such an intention. He returned to his mission station after staying with us for nine days,—not the happiest visit he had made to us.

Meanwhile, our college-days were coming near their end.

June 26, Sunday.—The last Sabbath in the college. The brethren spoke out their hearts in the meeting. W. offered prayer. I spoke that for the sake of the Kingdom of Heaven I would choose no place where I might be sent to. Charles spoke how he would work for the Kingdom's sake while engaged in a secular work, and he strongly maintained the importance of this phase of the Christian work. Then Francis, Edwin, Paul, Hugh followed, and told how much they were benefitted by our meetings during our college days. Y. gave us an exhortation. Z. laid stress upon the improvement of human hearts as *the* work of mankind. "Kahau" also had something to tell of his feeling. Frederick prayed at the close of the meeting. No such meeting during all our college days.

A most impressive meeting. The "church" which met through hot and cold, in love and hatred, during four long years, was now to be dissolved. Good-bye to the flour-barrel pulpit! We may in the days to come visit Boston, and worship in its Tremont Temple or Trinity Church; or roam through Europe, and hear the sacred mass at the Notre Dame in Paris, or at the famed cathedral in Cologne; may receive the papal benediction at St. Peter's, Rome; but the charm, the sacredness that attended thee when Frederick or Hugh passed the apostolic benediction from thee shall never be surpassed. Good-bye to the beloved water jug which drew us together to feastings both sacred and profane! Wine that we may partake from golden chalices shall never have that communing power with which the cool sparkling liquid as it came out of thy mouth knitted our heterogeneous hearts into one harmonious whole. Good-bye, ye blue blankets! The "pews" ye offered us were the comfortablest we shall ever have. Good-bye to the little "church" with all its "attractions" and childish experiments; its bickerings and insinuating prayers; its sweet talks and Sunday-afternoon feasts!

"Sweet Sabbath School! more dear to me
 Than fairest palace dome,
My heart e'er turns with joy to thee,
 My own dear Sabbath home.

"Here first my wilful, wandering heart,
 The way of life was shown;
Here first I sought the better part,
 And gained a Sabbath Home.

"Here Jesus stood with loving voice,
 Entreating me to come,
And make of Him my only choice,
 In this dear Sabbath Home."

"Sabbath Home! Blessed Home!
My heart e'er turns with joy to thee,
My own dear Sabbath Home."

July 9, Saturday.—The commencement day. Military drill at 1:15 P. M. Literary exercises begin at 2. The orations were as follows:

How Blessed is Rest after Toil,—Edwin.

The Importance of Morality in the Farmer, —Charles.

Agriculture as an Aid to Civilization,— Paul.

The Relation of Botany to Agriculture,— Francis.

The Relation of Chemistry to Agriculture, —Frederick.

Fishery as a Science,—Jonathan.

The distribution of diplomas by the president amidst loud applause. * * * * * * *
* * * * * * * * * * * * * *

I thank my Heavenly Father for all the honors of this day. The day for leaving the college is at hand; and as I think of the heavy responsibility I have to bear, how I must go among the sons of Satan (the world), I feel how strong should my faith become. Joys there are in my heart, but tears are not wanting. I only pray for the grace to serve my Heavenly Father with all humility.

The class entered the college with twenty-one. By illness and defection, we were reduced to twelve when we graduated. Seven of them were Christians, and they were the seven which occupied the first seven seats on the day of graduation. One main objection of the non-Christian part of the class against Christianity was that it did not allow them to study on Sundays. We the Christians accepted this Sabbath law; and though our examinations began always on Monday mornings, Sundays were days of rest to us, and Physics, Mathematics, or any thing that pertained to "flesh" was cast aside on holy days. But lo! at the close of our college days, when all our "marks" were summed up, we the Sabbath-keepers were given us the first seven seats in the class, were to make all the class speeches, and to carry away all the prizes but one! Thus we gave one more proof of the "practical advantage" of Sabbath-keeping, saying nothing of its intrinsic worth as a part of God's eternal laws.

Seven more were now added to the "contributable" force of Christians, and a true, veritable church might now be had. Had it not been our dream to have a real church,—not a toy church,—as soon as we went out to the world? Before we thought of having homes or making money, we thought of building a church. Let us, as our John said in his sermon, "disperse heathens as we do street-dogs," and conquer men, devils, and all, with our united force and courage.

"In the lexicon of youth, which fate reserves for a bright manhood, there is no such word as —fail."—Lytton.

CHAPTER IV.

A NEW CHURCH AND LAY-PREACHING.

As soon as we graduated from our college, each of us was offered a position with a salary of thirty dollars a month. We were taught in practical sciences, and were intended to develop the material resources of our country. We never have swerved from this aim. In Jesus of Nazareth we saw a man who was the Savior of mankind by being the son of a carpenter, and we his lowly disciples might be farmers, fishermen, engineers, manufacturers, and be at the same time preachers of the gospel of peace. Peter a fisherman and Paul a tent-maker were our examples. We never have construed Christianity as a hierarchy or ecclesiasticalism of any sort. We take it essentially as people's religion, and our being "men of the world" are of no obstacles whatever for our being preachers and missionaries. We believe, no more consecrated set of young men ever left a hall of learning than we when we left our science college. Our aim was spiritual, though our training and destinations were material.

After I finished my college-course, I made another visit to my home in the metropolis, this time all the "six brethren" coming up with me. Our stay in the city was thoroughly enjoyable. We had many invitations from missionaries, were lauded for what little we had done; were asked to speak of our experiences in their meetings. We

studied the construction of churches, and the ways of managing them, to apply them in our own church when we returned to our place. Though coming from the far north, from amidst primeval forests and bears and wolves, we found we were not the least intelligent among Christians. What we heard from the flour-barrel pulpit and talked about upon the blue blankets, were not the crudest thoughts when compared with the teachings and cultures of the metropolitan churches. On some points, indeed, we thought we had profounder and healthier views than our friends who were nurtured under the care of professional theologians.

I also carried on my missionary work among my friends and relatives, as I had done two years ago. The arch-heretic was my father, who with his learning and strong convictions of his own, was the hardest to approach with my faith. For three years I had been sending him books and pamphlets, and had written him constantly, imploring him to come to Christ and receive His salvation. He was a voracious reader and my books were not entirely ignored. But nothing could move him. He was a righteous man as far as social morality was concerned, and as is always the case with such a man, he was not one who felt the need of salvation most. At the close of my college course, I was again awarded with a little sum of money for my study and industry, and I thought of using it in the most profitable way possible. I prayed my God over it. Just then a thought occurred to me that I might take some presents to my parents; and no better articles were suggested to me for this purpose than the commentary on the Gospel of St. Mark, written by Dr. Faber, a German missionary in China.

The work was in five volumes, and as a product of sound and broad scholarship in the learnings of the people for whom it was intended, it was, and still is, very highly spoken of. It was written in unpointed Chinese, and I thought the difficulty of reading it, if not anything else, might whet my father's intellectual appetite to peruse it. I invested two dollars upon this work, and carried it in my trunk to my father. But alas! when I gave it to my father, no words of thanks or appreciation came from his lips, and all the best wishes of my heart met his coldest reception. I went into a closet and wept. The books were thrown into a box with other rubbishes; but I took out the first volume and left it on his table. In his leisure when he had nothing else to do, he would read a page or so, and again it went into the rubbish. I took it out again, and placed it upon his table as before. My patience was as great as his reluctance to read these books. Finally, however, I prevailed; he went through the first volume! He stopped to scoff at Christianity! Something in the book must have touched his heart! I did the same thing with the second volume as with the first. Yes, he finished the second volume too, and he began to speak favorably of Christianity. Thank God, he was coming. He finished the third volume, and I observed some change in his life and manners. He would drink less wine, and his behaviors toward his wife and children were becoming more affectionate than before. The fourth volume was finished, and his heart came down! "Son," he said, "I have been a proud man. From this day, you may be sure, I will be a disciple of Jesus." I took him to a church, and observed in him the convulsion of his whole nature. Everything he heard there moved him. The eyes that

were all masculine and soldierly were now wet
with tears. *He would not touch his wine any
more.* Twelve months more, and he was baptized.
He has studied the Scripture quite thoroughly,
and though he never was a bad man, he has been
a Christian man ever since. How thankful his
son was, the reader may judge for himself.—
Jericho fell, and the other cities of Canaan were
captured in succession. My cousin, my uncle, my
brothers, my mother, and my sister, all followed;
and for ten years, though the hand of Providence
hath dealt quite bitterly with us, and we have
been made to pass through many a deep water;
and though the faith we owned has made us repulsive in the eyes of the world, and much of the
comforts of life were to be given up for His name's
sake, I believe we are still second to no other
family in the land in our love and loyalty to our
Heavenly Master. Four years ago, another member was added to our family. She came to us as
a "heathen," but within a year, no woman was
more faithful to her Lord and Savior than she.
The good Lord removed her away from us after
she remained with us only a year and a half; but
her coming to us was her opportunity of finding
the Savior of her soul; and in Him confiding she
passed into His joy and bliss, after fighting right
nobly for her Master and country. Blessed is she
that sleepeth in the Lord, and blessed are we all
whose bond is in Him and is spiritual.

In autumn I returned once more to my field
of activity in the north. I took my younger
brother with me, as my family was poor, and I had
to unburden my parents, now that I became a
salaried man. I entered into a copartnership with
Edwin, Hugh, Charles, and Paul, and we together
kept a house. It was a continuation of our college

life, only with a little more of freedom and comfort in it than in our school dormitory.

Oct. 16, Sunday.—Mr. K. preaches in the
morning. We meet for the first time in our
new church in the South Street.

Mr. K. was a Presbyterian; not a college graduate, but a precious addition to our Christian community. He was a young man yet, but a man of
deep spirituality and extensive Christian experiences.

During our absence in the metropolis, O. the
"Missionary Monk" was industrious in finding a
house of worship for us. The place he hit upon
was one half of one building, and was procured
at the cost of two hundred and seventy dollars.
Our portion was about 30 x 36 feet, two stories
high, the roof shingled, and had a garden twice
as extensive as the house itself. It was built as
a tenement house, and a kitchen and fire-places
occupied a very large part of it. We rented the
two rooms in the upper story to help the general
expense of the church. The basement floor was
all fitted up for the church. Hugh ordered for us
six strong benches, and they were reserved for the
male part of the attendants. Ladies sat upon
straw mats, right in front of the pulpit which
consisted of an elevated platform and a table of
the simplest construction. But it was a decided
improvement upon the flour-barrel pulpit in our
"incipient church." When there were more attendants than these seats could hold, a large fire-
place which was a rectangular space cut into the
floor, was covered with pine boards; and blankets
spread upon them afforded seats for about ten
more. The house was crowded to its utmost ca-

pacity when fifty were present, and in winter-
time when a stove occupied a large space in front
of the pulpit so that a smoke-pipe hid the face of
the preacher from the view of the male population
of the congregation, every nook of the house was
filled by a human species of some kind, sitting
or reclining as it seemed most comfortable to
him. We had an organ too by this time. It was
given us by our friend, Rev. Mr. Den.,—not the
most perfect of its kind, but good enough for the
congregation it was to lead in the holy music. The
kind Providence provided a musician to play upon
this instrument in the person of one Mr. F., who
likewise was another valuable addition to the
church. As the ceiling was not more than ten feet
above the floor, the bellow of the organ swelled
by the chorus of fifty or more untutored voices
shook the building with discordant vibrations of
the most dreadful kind. The peace of our neighbors who lived next door to our wall was thus
much infringed upon, and their complaints which
were not altogether unjust were constant. And
woe was he, who boarded in the upper story! The
Sunday being the best day in the week, the brethren resorted to the house of worship from very
early in the morning; and not till the evening service was over at 10 p. m., and they all retired to
their nests, was the house free from human voices
of some kind. For the first time in our lives we
had a house of our own, and we used it as no
house was ever used. The eldest member of the
church who had recently joined us, called it an
"inn," where we might drop in at any time in our
life-journey to recuperate ourselves; and his
dropping-ins were as frequent as the moments of
rest he needed in his busy life in an advanced age.
It was a reading-room, a class-room, a committee-

room, a refreshment-room, and a club-room at the same time. Laughters that almost burst our diaphrams, sobs of penitence that touched our innermost hearts, arguments that wearied the biggest and soundest of our heads, and talks about markets and money-making schemes, were all heard in this most convenient of houses. Such was our church, and we never have seen the like of it in the whole world.

The work for union and independence was pushed on quite vigorously. Our Episcopalian brethren and sisters would give up their house of worship and join with us, and they brought with them their books and organ. The Church Missionary Society of England that helped them to buy the house would use it for its own purpose, and its "converts" would unite with us Methodists to pay back our debts to the Methodist Episcopal Mission. Both parties were to leave their respective denominations as soon as the debts were paid over, and the two to constitute themselves into one independent native church. The plan was agreed upon, and we on our part felt no difficulty about it. Only our outside friends discussed much about the propriety and feasibility of the plan, and the grave difficulties that might lie in our future. But we were blind as to our future, and thanks to our "blessed ignorance," the union was effected without any of the difficulties anticipated by our over-solicitous friends.

The constitution of the new church was the simplest that can be imagined. Our creed was the Apostle's Creed, and the church discipline was based upon the "Covenant of the Believers in Jesus," drawn up by our New England professor five years ago. The church was managed by a committee of five, one of them the treasurer. All common business was transacted by them; but when matters came up that the Covenant did not touch upon, such as the admission and dismission of members, the whole church was called together, and the votes of the two-thirds of the whole membership was required to carry them into effect. *The church required every one of its members to do something for it.* No one of them was to be idle, and if he could not do anything else, let him saw wood for our stove. Everybody was responsible for its growth and prosperity, and in this respect O. the "Missionary Monk" was no more responsible than our little "Miss Pine," the tiniest member of our church. Of course, not every one of us felt like preaching. So, O. the "Missionary Monk," W. the "Crocodile," John the "Episcopalian," and Jonathan occupied the pulpit in turn, and Mr. K. our Presbyterian friend helped us considerably in this line. Hugh was our faithful treasurer, and kept our accounts by the double-entry system of book-keeping. There was a special visiting committee, where our good Edwin appeared most conspicuously. The younger of our members formed a colporteur party, selling Bibles and tracts among the neighboring towns and villages. Many of us stayed mostly outside of the town, in exploring new lands, in surveying, in railroad construction, etc.; but they were all busy in Christian works as we at home. We will see further on how the whole machinery worked for the great aim we had in view.

Oct. 23.—We constitute a Y. M. C. A. Am appointed a vice-president.

Special works for young men became imperative, and a Y. M. C. A. was added to our works.

The idea we got while we were in the metropolis last summer.

Nov. 12.—The opening meeting of Y. M. C. A. The audience, about 60. Entertainment with tough rice after the meeting. A very prosperous gathering.

Our little church was filled to its utmost capacity. Tough rice is rice steamed with red beans, and is usually served up on occasions of congratulation. It tastes good, but our dyspeptic friends better not touch it, for only tough stomachs can bear it.—I remember I was one of the speakers of the day. My subject was: "The Relation of the Scallop-Shell to Christianity." The point was to reconcile Geology with the Book of Genesis; and the scallop-shell was especially chosen for this purpose, as our species *Pecten yessoensis* was the commonest mollusk on our coast, and its shells were abundantly found as fossils. Such words and phrases as "Evolution," "the Struggle for Existence," and "the Survival of the Fittest" were being heard in our circles; and a blow was found necessary upon the atheistic evolutionists who were beginning to make some figures in our country about that time. My subject sounded odd, and the boys heard me well.

Nov. 15, Tuesday.—Meet with W. and O. at 3 P. M. and consult about the church. The whole congregation meets at 4, and discusses about the future of the church.—One hundred dollars ($100) in U. S. gold sent by Prof. Dr. C. is received.

A preliminary meeting of three members of the

committee was followed by the general gathering
of the whole congregation. Now that we set sail
on the boisterous sea of the practical life, we
found the human existence to be a more real and
serious affair than we had imagined in our class-
rooms. Things did not move as we willed and
planned. Not every one of us was in red-hot earnestness about the church, and some flaggings of
interest were recognizable in certain quarters.
We had already run into a debt of four hundred
dollars, and the general expense of the church
was not small, though we paid nothing to our
preachers. How to meet all these difficulties was
the question to be decided in the meeting. No
good thoughts were coming. Only let us be prepared to unstring our purses, for we might be required to give all we had for the cause. We
separated with sighs and anxieties.—O. the "Missionary Monk" returns to his nest, and behold,
something is waiting for him. A cheque for one
hundred dollars in U. S. gold sent for the church
by the originator of the "Covenant of the Believers in Jesus," sent away from his home in New
England! Jehovah-jireh,—the Lord will provide! Lift up your heads, ye brethren! We are
not forsaken by the Father in Heaven. The good
news spreads through the congregation, and hope
revives within us.

Dec. 18, Sunday.—Severe snow-storm. I
preached. Much distressed by the snow
being driven into the church.

Our cheap wooden structure was not snow-
proof, and our ladies' quarter was not available
for use on that day. The sledge that carried them
stuck in the snow, and they had a hard time in

reaching their home. We forget not such a meeting in such a weather.

Dec. 29, Thursday.—Busy through the whole afternoon. All things were ready before dusk. The meeting began at 6 P. M. Brethren and sisters to the number of 30 were present. The best meeting we have had in S. All spoke of their hearts, and enjoyed the evening freely till half-past 9 o'clock.

The usual Christmas festival was postponed till this day, when all the members of the church could be back in the town. This was essentially a Christian gathering; no more wrestling of Dharmas and dancing of a savage as in the Christmas of two years ago. The joy we felt this evening was truly spiritual. The year in whole was a successful one, and the works we had accomplished were not small. Sweet were the pleasures after toils!

Jan. 1, 1882, Sunday.—All meet in the church in afternoon and express their feelings. Letters from Messrs. D. and H. Much distressed.

The fact was, while we were saying Happy-New-Year's to one another, rejoicing in God's blessings for the year that had just gone by, two letters were received by us, one from Rev. Mr. H. our beloved missionary friend, and the other from Rev. Mr. D. The latter was a short, incisive letter, stating briefly that he could not very well give his consent to our plan of forming an independent church, and asking us to pay back to him by telegram any part of the money which his church had forwarded to us to build a house of worship. His letter was construed as his avowed dissent from our procedure, which was enforced by a requirement to square our accounts with his church if we would separate ourselves from his denomination. And such a construction of his letter was not wholly unreasonable, for our financial state must have been well known to him, and his words were too few to carry any sentiments of real sympathy in our motive. If the Methodist Episcopal Mission lent us money that we might start its denominational church in our place, we should never have asked its aid. Our independence was not intended as a revolt against Methodism, but as an expression of our real attachment to our heavenly Master, and of the highest sentiment of our love to our nation. We borrowed the money, though the mission said it would be given us. We were all young then, and our animal spirit was high too. "Let's pay it at once. Prof. C.'s money is still untouched, and let the church chest be emptied to the last cent to clear our debt!" said one. "Agreed! Pay on!" all rejoined. Jonathan was charged to consult with Hugh the treasurer, and to send to Mr. D. by a telegraphic money order all the available sum of money in the church treasury. I believe nothing knitted the two Christian bodies of the place more firmly than this very unwelcome letter on the first day of January.

Jan. 6.—Send $200 to Rev. Mr. D. by telegraphic money order.

We tried to comply with Mr. D.'s requirement at once by paying him all our debt to his denomination. But this we could not do with all our possible means. We had been taxing our brethren pretty heavily, and we could not exact any more from them. Prof. C.'s money formed the main bulk of the present installment. We were not very happy in letting go the money so soon after it reached us.

Jan. 7.—Busy in arranging for the Dedication Service of to-morrow.

Jan. 8.—The Dedication Service of the S. Church begins at 2 P. M.

The attendance about 50. To-day we dedicate this church to God. May His glory shine forth in this district from this place.

The common burden we had to bear knitted our hearts together, and we might now enter into a formal union, and publicly dedicate to God the church of our own. The little wooden building shook with the hallelujahs of fifty united voices, —woe to our poor neighbors! Our organ, whose two keys were out of tune, bellowed forth the loudest anthems at the touch of Mr. F.'s fingers. Unto the name of the Most High God we dedicate this humble dwelling, the best and utmost of all we can offer! Let this be the veritable Shekinah, and His presence be as real in it as in the gorgeous temple of the wise son of David. He liketh a broken and contrite heart under whatever garbs it dwells; and the church that He liketh best has no need of pipe-organs, stained glass windows, and baptismal fonts. A clear January sun shined upon plain unvarnished benches through two windows partly covered by curtains of the coarsest texture, as our good O. passed his benediction upon the humble crowd that bowed in gratitude. We could almost hear in the dry bracing wintry air the voice of Him who said, "Of a truth I say unto you, that this poor widow hath cast in more than they all." Luke XXI, 2.

Feb. 16, Thursday.—Meet with O. W., and John to frame rules for the S. Church. Monday, Tuesday, Thursday and Friday are fixed as the days for meeting.

Now that we dedicated our house of worship, some written forms of the church regulations became imperative. Four of the members of the Executive Committee were empowered to prepare drafts of such rules. We were to consider what should rule this most unique of Christian churches,—to preserve all that were essential in Christianity, and to adapt them to our new surroundings. For seven days the discussions continued, which resulted in a rough frame-work of the church organizations. The meeting was opened with prayers and closed with prayers. We were awfully earnest, and disposed of articles after articles as we surrounded a little fire-place and heard a tea-kettle singing for us a resonant music with its steam-jets. Jonathan's dashing thoughts were tempered by O.'s cool judgement; and John's opportune ideas were corrected by W.'s legality to adjust them to the time. The whole now needed the consent of the church council to become effective.

March 6.—Removed to the church-building.

They offered me a room in the upper story of the church, but not for nothing. I was charged to sweep the meeting-place, to look after the church-library, and to take up all the duties of a janitor and a sexton; and to pay to the treasury two dollars a month as my room-rent. I have not seen such a convenient church-officer anywhere else. From this day, my room became a regular resorting place of the brethren.

March 13.—Made a mutual pledge to clear the church debt by the October of this year.

Our debt-paying must not be indefinitely delayed. Let every body make up his mind to pay his portion within the specified time. Suppose you give up your European restaurant for ten months; that will help you to pay half your portion. Suppose you go with your old jacket and pants until the next year; that will enable you to fill up your share of the common burden. The net income of each of us was twenty-five dollars a month, and we were to pay a whole month's salary by the October next.

Sept. 2—Set out to the A-mill with Brother Ts. I preached in the evening.

Sept. 3.—Left the A-mill in morning. Stopped at Mr. H.'s and preached. The outlook in the Mill is hopeful.

The opening of a preaching station in the A—mill is one of the most memorable episodes in our church history, and one that illustrates the methods of our united Christian work better than any other work we had accomplished. The mill was about fifteen miles from our place, up in a mountain district, where the Government had recently introduced an American turbine wheel to reduce huge pine forests to shingles and timbers. A carriage road was to be constructed from our place to the new mill, and surveyors were sent out to reconnoitre for the new highway. It so happened that our U. the "Good-Natured" was the chief-surveyor in this expedition, and while he was engaged in his work, he did what he could to introduce the Bible and Christianity to the little colony that was formed around the mill. As soon as the route was determined upon, the final survey was entrusted to Hugh, our church-treasurer, who during his stay in the mountain succeeded in bringing one very precious soul to Christ, O. nicknamed the "Apodal." Now that the road was surveyed, the man who was appointed to construct it was Mr. H., another member of our church. He too labored for Christ among his colleagues, and his words in the dead silence of the primeval forest were not without effects. Before the road was fairly finished another worthy soul was won for the Master. Meanwhile the seed which U. the "Good-Natured" had sown in the mill was sprouting and making good growth. The people there were impatient for the opening of the new road, and they sent us words to come and preach the Gospel to them. So I was sent with Brother T. on this errand, and we were the first that trod the road which was reconnoitred by a Christian, surveyed by a Christian, and built by a Christian. Before a single piece of timber was carried over this road, the feet of those that carried the glad tidings of Peace were upon it. It was essentially a "Christian" road, and "the Way" we called it. "Every valley shall be exalted, and every mountain and hill shall be made low," that the King of Glory may come in.

Sept. 23, Saturday.—A national holiday.
Not a speck of cloud in the sky. At 1 P. M. all
gathered at the church, and together proceeded to the museum ground. There were
poem-makings, tea-parties, and ring-throw-
ing. All enjoyed the day completely.

This was a "field day" for our church-members,
which we repeated usually twice a year,—in
spring and in autumn. While we were yet "heathens," we had such *fete champetre*, with poison-
ous drinks to cause unnatural exhilarations, and
"devil-ings," as plays were called where one of
us nominated a "devil" was to catch any one who
strayed out of the "heaven," and he who was
thus caught was to be a devil himself. But the
new religion had ameliorated our tempers, and
though we enjoyed open air and innocent plays
as much as ever before, we substituted poem-
makings and tea-drinkings to "devil-ings" and
alcohol-drinkings; and the pleasures we derived
from such a change we found to be far superior
to what our unconverted friends were still indulging in. I have already told my readers how we
knitted our hearts together in winter-time around
one common iron kettle. Either when "snow-
bound," or on the "museum ground," we counted
much upon these social gatherings for the effect-
iveness of our united church-work.

Between this and the end of the year, nothing
worth mentioning came in our experiences. I
was busy both in religious and secular works.
The condition of the church was fairly settled
by this time. As we had pledged early this year,
the money to be paid back to the M. E. Mission
was gradually coming in. Not everybody paid his

portion very willingly, but pay he did nevertheless. Near the close of the year, John and I were in the metropolis, and we were entrusted with the money to square our accounts with the mission.

Dec. 28.—Drew money from the Bank, and paid it to Rev. Mr. S.

S   Church is Independent.

Joys inexpressable and indescribable!

The result of two years' economy and industry was our freedom from the church-debt, and well we might leap with joy and thanksgiving. Here is our *Magna Charta:*

"$181.31.   Metropolis, Dec. 28, 1882.
Rec'd of Mr. Jonathan X., the sum of One Hundred and Eighty One Dollars and Thirty One Sen, being the Balance due the M. E. Mission, on account of a Loan ($698.40) to the S. Christians, to assist them in building a church, in the year 1881.   J. S."

We were thankful that we now owed no man anything, except in our sense of gratitude for the help extended toward us, enabling us to use the money *without interest* for two years.

They do err who think that our church-independence was intended as an open rebellion against the denomination to which we once belonged. It was an humble attempt to reach the one great aim we had in view; namely, to come to the full consciousness of our own powers and capabilities (God-given), and to remove obstacles in the way of others seeking God's Truth for the salvation of their souls. He only knows how much he really can do who knows how to rely upon himself. A dependent man is the most helpless being in this universe. Many a church complains of its lack of means whose members could afford to spend much upon unnecessary luxuries. Many a church can stand upon its own feet if but its members could forego some of their "hobbies." *Independence is the conscious real-ization of one's own capabilities;* and I believe this to be the beginning of the realization of many other possibilities in the field of human activity. This is the kindliest and most philosophic way of looking at independence of any kind. To stig-matize it as a rebellion, or as an instigation of the unthinking mass by a few ambitious men, is not generous, especially in a Christian, whose peculiarity should be that he "thinketh no evil."

Dec. 29.—The members of the S. Church who were present in the metropolis assemble at Francis' at 1 P. M. Together we went to the "Plum Restaurant" in the Morning Grass Park, and supped together, and celebrated the Independence of our Church.

This was our first "Fourth of July." I think there were with us Francis, W. the "Crocodile," and T. the "Pterodactyl." The last in his usual savage style swallowed the contents of the first cup of soup that was brought to him; and after-ward asked the waitress what was in the soup. Upon being answered that there were some tiny clam-shells in it, he confessed that he was so glad of church-independence that he sent everything that was in the cup through his oesophagus with-out the process of mastication taking place upon it in his ante-pharyngeal chamber. I think the real explanation of it was he was really very hungry.

With the independence of my church, I took my farewell of it. The church needs a separate history for itself, to describe it in all its bearings upon the great question of the evangelization of nations. Four years ago, I paid a visit to my old home-church, and to my most grateful satisfaction, I found it in a very much more prosperous state than when I left it thirteen years ago. I found O. the "Missionary Monk" the same faithful pastor, *receiving not a cent for his whole-souled devotion to his church,* earning a livelihood by teaching in the college where I graduated. The members numbered some 250. They engaged two salaried evangelists, had a prosperous Y. M. C. A., originated and sustained a strong temperance union. During 1885, the year that witnessed the greatest activity among the Christians of all denominations in our land, the amount of contribution *per capita* of some of the more influential churches were as follows:

Independent Native Church.................$7.32
Congregational Church 2.63
Presbyterian and Dutch Reformed........ 2.00
Methodist Church 1.74
English Episcopal Church................ 1.74

The comparison speaks too well for our own church. They built a new church costing some one thousand dollars, and though it looked somewhat like a "nigger church" which I saw in Virginia, it was a decided improvement upon that "one-half of one building" whose janitor and sexton I once was. A new organ they had too, with keys all in order. They were speaking of erecting a new stone-church before long. It is really the only church in the whole country, which is independent in the full significance of that term. Not only financially, but ecclesiastically and theologically, they were carrying on their Christian works upon their own responsibilities, with the happiest results. They have a system and principles peculiar to their own, and we believe the Lord wants them to retain those peculiarities as sacred. They have a special mission to fulfill, let no one disturb them in their simplicity and contentment.

CHAPTER V.

OUT INTO THE WORLD.—SENTIMENTAL CHRISTIANITY.

"Therefore, behold, I will allure her, and bring her into the wilderness, and speak comfortably unto her. And I will give her vineyards from thence, and the valley of Achor for a door of hope; and she shall sing there, as in the days of her youth, and as in the day when she came up out of the land of Egypt. And it shall be at that day, saith the Lord, that thou shalt call me Ishi; and shall call me no more Baali."—Hoshea, II, 14, 15, 16.

So my Lord and Husband must have said to Himself when He drove me from my peaceful home-church. He did this by creating a vacuum in my heart. Nobody goes to a desert who has his all in his home. Nature abhors vacuum, and human heart abhors it more than anything else in the Universe. I descried in myself an empty space which neither activity in religious works, nor success in scientific experiments, could fill. What the exact nature of that emptiness was, I was not able to discern. May be, my health was getting poor, and I yearned after repose and easier tasks. Or, as I was rapidly growing into my manhood, that irresistible call of nature for companionship might have made me feel so haggard and empty. At all events, a vacuum there was, and it must be filled *somehow* with *some-*

thing. I thought *something* there was in this vague universe which could make me feel happy and contented; but I had no idea whatever of what that something was. Like a pigeon that was deprived of its cerebrum by the knife of a physiologist, I started, not knowing whither and wherefore, but because stay I could not. From this time on, my whole energy was thrown into this *one* task of filling up this vacuum.

April 12, 1883.—Depression; no spirit.

April 22.—Repented my past sins deeply, and felt my total inability to save myself by my own efforts.

Incontestable signs that the good Angel was coming down occasionally to disturb the stagnant pool of my soul, that healing might come to it some future day.

May 8.—The Third Great Gathering of Christians opens at 9 A. M. in the New Prosperity St. Presbyterian Church. I represented the S. Church. Prayers and business in morning. Reports on the state of the Faith throughout the land, in afternoon. The believers number 5,000 in all. The meeting adjourned at 6 P. M.

This was some twenty years after Christianity was first introduced into my country. The believers numbered 5,000 among 40,000,000 of the entire population;—a small flock indeed, but fired with holy ambition to leaven the whole mass of ignorance and superstition around them *within a quarter of a century!* This sanguine hope was based upon a calculation made 'by one Mr. T., an elderly brother of the most optimistic type of mind, that even if each of the five-thousand Christians be so lazy as to lead but a single soul to Christ in one year, the congregation ought to swell to many times the number of living souls in the whole land within that short period. The fact was the increase in the number of new converts had been from 25 to 33 per cent. for the last three or four years, and the coolest heads among us did not doubt 25 per cent. as the average increase for the coming quarter of a century. Writing now, however, ten years after this memorable meeting, I have a sad task of telling my readers that history has proved quite otherwise from what we expected or prophesied. They say there are now 35,000 Christians throughout the land, and that the yearly average of increase is rapidly falling. Yes, a nation cannot be converted in a day! Let it be! Our aim is *qualitative* as well as *quantitative.* A man who for the first time in his life saw a baby grow, thought that as it gained a pound in a week, therefore it ought to be as big as a good-sized elephant when it would get to be thirty years of age. Either our own laziness or God's own wisdom has always kept the numerical value of the believers at comparatively low figures.

Be the future whatever it might, our dream on that day was resplendent with glory. It was unanimously agreed upon that a veritable Pentecost did set in after it had ceased to be a human experience for over eighteen centuries. And there was every sign that such was truly the case. First, there was much groaning for sins. Everybody wept, and he was considered a block-heart

who could not weep on such an occasion. Some
miraculous conversions were reported. It was
said that a group of children of a mission school
were so endowed with the power of spirit that
they captured a poor Buddhist pilgrim in a street,
prayed with him, and argued with him, stripped
his sacerdotal robe from him, and compelled him
to own Jesus as his Savior. A young man, conspicuous among his fellows for his stammering
tongue, was said to have had the restraint removed from him, and to have preached with all
the fire and freedom of the Apostle Peter. And
what was more, we had among us a Corean, a
high-born representative of that hermit nation!
He was baptized a week before this, and was with
us in all the dignity of his native attire. He
too prayed in his own language, not intelligible
to us except his closing Amen, but forcible because his presence and unintelligibility made the
scene still more Pentecostal. We only needed a
physical tongue of fire to make it entirely so;
but this we furnished with our own imaginations.
We all felt something miraculous and stupendous
coming over us. We even doubted whether the
sun was still shining over our heads.

May 9.—Meeting of the delegates in the
Morning Grass Presbyterian Church at 8 A.
M. The subject of discussion, "the Free
Burial."

The gathering continues. Something must be
done with a law still extant in the country, which
enforced the signature of a heathen priest before a corpse was committed to earth. Legally
such a thing as Christian burial was not allowed;
and such was procured only by the connivance

of presiding priests, or in many actual cases, by
bribing them. I for one maintained that the
dead might be buried by the dead without any
detriment to the soul that once dwelt in it, and
that since our God was the God of the living,
He would not require from us any special mode
of disposing of our lifeless bodies. But those
of my brethren otherwise-minded on this subject
carried the day, and the majority vote decided
upon making a special petition to the government
to change the said law. This was thought to be
the beginning of a great movement which must
ultimately be taken up for bestowal of religious
liberty upon the nation. Events proved, however,
that legalism was fruitless in all cases. What
clamorings for right could not obtain, time and
progress of thought freely gave. The nation has
now a Constitution with religious liberty as a
conspicuous clause.

May 12.—The Great Meeting closes. It had
wonderful effects. Churches revived, con-
sciences tried, and love and union considerably strengthened. Very Pentecostal in its
general character.

All in all, the meetings were profitable to us
all. Enthusiasm ran so high that after-meetings
were continued for one week more. To me the
scene was one which I had never seen before in
my life. The so-called "revival" set in upon the
metropolitan churches, and to me who was trained
a little in Mental Physiology, the movement appeared somewhat insanoid. Carpenter in his
Mental Physiology tells us of a case of a whole
monastery which went to imitating a cat's mew-
ing, after one of its inmates, a nun, contracted this

propensity. Many at least of the phenomena of revivals could be explained as abnormal actions of the sympathetic nerves. But as the movement was fanned and supported by the highest of church-dignitaries and reverend gentlemen, I suppressed my skepticism, and allowed myself to be swayed over by the prevailing sentiment of the hour. When I saw and heard many who spoke of the joy that came over their souls by the mysterious influence of what they could never explain, but no less real on that account,—the joy, they told us, exceeding that the eye hath ever seen, or the ear hath ever heard of,—my science was carried over by my desire to have the similar joy myself. Having been taught by a fiery Methodist preacher how to obtain this unspeakable gift of spirit, I applied myself right earnestly at the work, focusing my mental vision upon my "deceitful heart," meanwhile blinding my eyes to Huxley, Carpenter, and Gegenbaur, as to visions which were infernal in their origin. But alas! the welcome voice "thy sins are forgiven thee" was not to be caught either by my physical or mental or spiritual tympanum. After three consecutive days of groanings and beatings of my breast, I was the same son of depravity as ever before. To me was denied the much envied privilege of showing myself before my fellow-Christians as a special object of heaven's favor, full of hope and of joy. My disappointment was indeed sore. Shall I explain away "revivals" as a sort of hypnotism, phenomena psycho-electrical in their origin; or is the profundity of my depravity the real cause of my non-susceptibility to them? Yes, the world was not created in a single day or week, and I may yet hope to be recreated through processes more "natural" than those prescribed by my Methodist friend.

With the daily and weekly increase of friends and acquaintances among the believers, my religion was fast inclining toward sentimentalism. Feastings upon religious talks were often carried to excess, and we thought more about Christian tea-parties and dinner-parties than of the grave responsibilities of conquering the dominion of darkness around us. Fresh from my country church, with childish innocence and credulity, I plunged myself into the Turkish-bath-society of metropolitan Christianity, to be lulled and shampooed by hymns sung by maidens, and sermons that offended nobody. God's kingdom was imagined to be one of perfect repose and constant free exchange of good wishes, where tea-parties and love-makings could be indulged in with the sanction of the religion of free communions and free love. Missionaries will pay all the arrears of church expenses, and they too will fight out Buddhism and other obnoxious superstitions around us. But we, dear brethren, who bow no more to wood and stones, and sweet sisters with woman's right bestowed upon you by the new faith,—let us be going to tea-parties and church-sociables, and there sing "Blest be the tie that binds," and pray and weep and dream and rejoice. Away with that Confucian superstition that forbids children of two sexes above seven years of age to sit together in one and the same room, and with that Buddhist nonsense that requires from womanhood modesty and subjection so debasing to her noble sex. Love is a mutual affair, and heaven itself cannot interfere in the communion of youthful hearts prompted by this holy and all pervading influence!

O Christian Freedom, thou that withstood black famine and Spanish halberds in the flooded fortress of Leyden, that hissed upon the faggots of Smithfield, and bled upon the top of Bunker Hill, how often hast thou lent thy name to Sirens of Destruction born, and to Jupiter's amorous son! O may thy name be cautiously held back from the people who to Sinai are not first led, there to learn the majesty of the Law, before thou liftest them above the Law. Thy tidings glad were not meant for those who from restraints are vainly striving to flee, but for those chosen children of God, who in their anxious efforts to conform themselves to the Law, are helped by Thee to make the Law their will.

But when the numerical increase of converts in geometric progression is had in view by the messengers of the Gospel (though not an altogether unpardonable weakness of humanity), this stern idea of Freedom must not be very conspicuously placed before heathens. Hence the more or less ✓ laxity of practical morality among the converts thus recruited, and the hedonistic view of the freedom of spirit engendered among them.

March 14.—Read John Howard's Life with tears. Gave me great joy and consolation.

Failure in putting off my old Adamic skin at once drove me to find a consolation in the works of my own hand. And why not? Sentimental Christianity, like all other pleasures of senses, soon becomes insipid, and something more real and substantial is needed to keep a hungering soul at rest. "Is not practical charity the essence of Christianity," I began to ask myself. Certainly the immortal Buddha taught it as the very first of the four conditions for a man to enter the bliss of Nirvana. "What doth it profit, my brethren,"

so runs the weighty admonition of the royal
Apostle, "though a man say he hath faith, and
have not works? can faith save him?" Prayer-
meeting sentimentalisms and camp-meeting
psycho-electricities,—to what do they all amount
if not a single beggar has his belly filled thereby!
We used to give something solid and substantial
to wayside beggars when we paid our monthly
pilgrimage to our family-idols; but now that we
are converted to Christianity, we give nothing
but empty words to them. Such should not be,
my soul! As well a man catch a bream by bait-
ing his hook with a lobster, as a Christian enter
his heaven by dealing out winds of doctrines to
others. So I bought a little volume of the life of
John Howard written in English, and read and
re-read it with intense applications. "Such I shall
be," I said to myself, and I already imagined myself visiting all the penitentiaries of the world,
and dying at last while attending a fever-stricken
soldier. I also bought Charles Loring Brace's
"Gesta Christi," and found therein all that I
needed to convince me of the mission appropriate
for all true lovers of Christ. Though my idea of
Christian philanthropy has considerably changed
since then, the healthy influence of that New York
philanthropist upon the whole turn of my thought
and action is above all I can thank for.

June 6.—Left my lodging at 7:30 A. M.
Hired a boat at Port "Barbaric," and rowed
by four sailors, started for Cape Eagle to
study the neighboring sea-bottom. Stopped
at Hotel No. 11 in the Cape.

Once more in the Government employ, I was
sent out upon another scientific tour. This boat-

excursion during my stay in the little island of
S.—I specially remember as one when my temperance principle was put to quite a test. Still
tenaciously holding teetotalism as a part of my
Christian profession, I was scrupulously careful
not to touch the fiery liquid even if presented with
the most plausible reasons. As was hinted in a
former chapter, liquor-drinking forms a large
part of my national etiquettes, and to refuse
cordial cups is to refuse friendship and intimacy
solicited by one who presents them. And in no
other respect was Christianity a sorer thorn in my
flesh than in this constant fear of offending my
hosts when asked to partake of friendly draughts
of rice-beer. But the sacred pledge was not to be
forgone; so I persisted.

But a new trial was to be met at Cape Eagle,
for there at the utmost outskirts of civilization,
in a lonely fishing-village, "Hotel No. 11" was the
only house where travelers could find shelter at
night. And the host of the hotel was a con-
firmed drunkard, known throughout the whole
island as a Bacchus out of a beer-barrel born, and
whose admiration of the "holy water" was so
intense, and generosity toward his fellowmen so
jealously strong, that he would not allow any
mortal to pass a night under his roof without
sharing his elixir with him, and so adding one
more praise to the liquid that makes even gods to
rejoice. I was told that not a single person had
ever been known having courage to refuse the cup
when presented by his imperious hand, and that
this once at least I must put my teetotalism
by, if to the Cape I must go. My answer was:
"To the Cape I will go, but the drink I will not
touch." The little community that sent me out
was taken up with quite a fuss over the possible

outcome of a singular contest which was to take place between the upholders of the two diametrically opposite principles.

It was near the dusk of the day when I found myself at the gate of the much-dreaded "Hotel No. 11." The man who received me was some sixty years of age, haggard in appearance and short in stature, and wearing unmistakable signs of alcoholic medications of a life-time. I at once recognized in him the man so much spoken of throughout the island, and I was on my guard to behave myself accordingly. All the courtesies and welcomes of country hotel-keepers were entirely lacking in him, and I had to tell him of my official dignity before he agreed to grudge me a shelter for the night. After bathing and tea-drinking as usual, the matron of the house came to me, and asked me to "drink" before the supper. "Not a drop of the liquor, madam," I resolutely replied, assured that everything depended upon my first answer. She retired, and in a moment a young man appeared with a wooden stand, upon which were arranged white rice, vegetables and boiled shell-fish in due order. The day's exposure to sun and sea prepared my stomach for the speedy consumption of the plain supper. Then I waited for the real tug of the battle, when the old man would appear with a bottle in his withered arm. But it was not so to be. Soon a bed was prepared for me, and without any interruption I passed a sweet peaceful night. I thought my friends had merely frightened me, and the whole story of the old man's demoniacal habits was manufactured solely for this purpose.

The next morning after breakfast, I was again on my boat. My men on their oars, my anxious inquiry was about the eventlessness of the night

before. The whole mystery was now explained
to me. "The hotel-keeper was the same old man,"
said one of my men, "but it was you, my young
lord, who made the whole household so quiet last
night. He told his servants that he himself would
not drink for the fear that he might disturb the
young guest, at which the whole family was taken
with surprise, though not thankless on that account; for now for the first time since they entered the service of the drunkard master, the
night was to be without murmurings and brawl-
ings and other confusions." "Yes," said another
of my men, "the matron expressed her thanks for
the blessings of the night before. She said this
morning before we left the house, that the sleep
she enjoyed last night was the most delicious she
ever had." "Victory!" I cried out; and as I was
preaching to my men the horrors of the drinking
habit and the power of brave resistence, heaven
itself seemed to have joined in our triumph, for
soon the wind veered to our back, and distending
our full-stretched sail, wafted us proudly into the
harbor, there to tell my anxious friends of the
victory that crowned my steadfast denial,—Bacchus himself disarmed of his bottles, and a peaceful repose given to his innocent household.

But the vacuum in my soul was not to be ob-
literated by a few such experiences, the more so
as Sentimental Christianity, itself a vacuity, had
made it larger and more conspicuous than ever
before. Failing to find the desired satisfaction in
my own land, I, Rasselas-like, thought of extending my search to a land differently constituted
from my own, even to Christendom, where,—
Christianity having had undisputed power and
influence for hundreds of years, must, I imagined,
be found Peace and Joy in a measure inconceiv-

able to us of heathen extraction, and easily procurable by any sincere seeker after the Truth. The pain of separation from dear ones, the expense almost unbearably heavy to one of my circumstances, and above all, that saddest of all human experiences, roaming a penniless exile in a strange land,—all these were to be cheerfully borne that I might win the coveted prize, and so make my existence endurable.

But the search after personal satisfaction was not the only motive that impelled me to take this bold step. The land which gave me birth requires from every one of its youths some unstinted contributions to its honor and glory; and that I might be a faithful son of my soil, I needed experience, knowledge, and observations extending beyond the limit of my country. To be a *man* first, and then a *Patriot,* was my aim in going abroad.

By the willing sacrifice of my poor family, and the result of my economy during the past three years, I provided myself with enough means to secure passage across the broadest of oceans, trusting all the rest in the hand of Him who would not suffer me to die with hunger in a strange land. My good father, who was already a devout Christian, sent me out with cheer and God-speed, giving me, together with all that he had, his heart and love for his beloved son, expressed in a native stanza of his own production:

> "Where I see not, Jehovah seeth;
> Where I hear not, Almighty heareth.
> Go my son, be not 'fraid;
> He thy help, there, as here."

The solemnity of the hour of separation called forth from us a nature which dogmas could not suppress. After my father's heart-rending prayers for the watchful care of Providence over his son, he took me to the ancestral shrine which we still kept, and there bade me to address myself to the soul of my departed grandfather before I would cross the threshold of my house on this hazardous voyage. "Had thy grandsire been here," he said in tears, "what an amazement it must have been for him that his grandson should go to the people whom he regarded as utter barbarians!" I bowed my head, and my soul, directed alike to my Heavenly Father and to the departed spirits of my ancestors, engaged in a sort of meditation at once a prayer and a retrospection. Our dogmatic teachers might have frowned upon us for our conduct so Buddhistic or Popish; but it was not time for us to argue then. We loved our God, our country, and our forefathers, and we remembered them all on this solemn occasion.

Love of country, like all other loves, is in its best and highest at the time of separation. That strange Something, which, when at home, is no more to us than a mere grouping of rills and valleys, mountains and hills, is now transformed to that living Somebody,—Nature etherialized into a spirit;—and like as a woman speaks to her children, it summons us to noble deeds,—a Cornelia sending forth young Gracchii that they might live and die worthy of their illustrious mother. The yonder imperial peak that hangs majestically against the western sky, white-capped with eternal snow,—is that not her chaste brow, the inspirer of the nation's heart? The pine-clad hills that encircle the peak, and golden fields that in its bottom lie,—is that not the bosom that suckled me, and the knee that took me up? And the waves dashing at its foot, and breaking into foamy sprays,—are they not pearl-set frills that fringe her gown as she strides forth in her majestic march? A mother so pure, so noble and lovely,—shall not her sons be loyal to her? I left her coast, and soon I was upon board a ship, flying a color of another nation, and manned by men of other races. The ship begins to move,—farewell to the mother-land,—and after few hours of tossing, only the tip of the peak imperial can be seen. "All to the deck," we cry; "one more homage to the dear, dear land." Below the billowy horizon she is setting; and our hearts with deep solemnity catch the words of the Quaker poet, and say,

"Land of lands, for thee we give,
Our hearts, our pray'rs, our service free;
For thee thy sons shall nobly live,
And at thy need shall die for thee."

CHAPTER VI.

THE FIRST IMPRESSIONS OF CHRISTENDOM.

That I looked upon Christendom and English-speaking peoples with peculiar reverence was not an altogether inexcusable weakness on my part. It was the same weakness that made the Great Frederick of Prussia a slavish adorer of everything that was French. I learnt all that was noble, useful, and uplifting through the vehicle of the English language. I read my Bible in English. Barnes' commentaries were written in English, John Howard was an Englishman, and Washington and Daniel Webster were of English descent. A "dime-novel" was never placed in my hand, and as for slangs,—the word itself I did not learn till long after my living among English-speaking people. My idea of Christian America was lofty, religious, Puritanic. I dreamed of its templed hills, and rocks that rang with hymns and praises. Hebraisms, I thought, to be the prevailing speech of the American commonality, and cherub and cherubim, hallelujahs and amens, the common language of its streets.

I was often told upon good testimony that money is all in all in America, and that it is worshipped there as Almighty Dollar; that the race prejudice is so strong there that the yellow skin and almond-shaped eyes pass for objects of derision and dog-barking; etc., etc. But for me to credit such statements as anything near the truth was utterly impossible. The land of Patrick Henry and Abraham Lincoln, of Dorothea Dix and Stephen Girard,—how could it be a land of mammon-worship and race-distinction! I thought I had different eyes to judge of the matter—so strong was my confidence in what I had read and heard about the superiority of the Christian civilization over that of the Pagan. Indeed, the image of America as pictured upon my mind was that of a Holy Land.

At the day-break of Nov. 24, 1884, my enraptured eyes first caught the faint views of Christendom. Once more I descended to my steerage-cabin, and there I was upon my knees—the moment was too serious for me to join with the popular excitement of the hour. As the low Coast Range came clearer to my views, the sense of my dreams being now realized overwhelmed me with gratitude, and tears trickled rapidly down my cheeks. Soon the Golden Gate was passed, and all the chimneys and mast-tops now presented to my vision appeared like so many church-spires pointing toward the sky. We landed—the company of some twenty young men—and were hackneyed to a hotel owned by an Irishman who was known to show special kindness to men of my nation. As my previous acquaintance with the Caucasian race had been mostly with missionaries, the idea stuck close to my mind; and so all the people whom I met in the street appeared to me like so many ministers fraught with high Christian purpose, and I could not but imagine myself as walking among the congregation of the First-born. It was only gradually, very gradually, that I unlearnt this childish notion.

Yes, Hebraism in one sense at least I found to be a common form of speech in America. First of all, everybody has a Hebrew name, and even horses are christened there. The words which we have never pronounced without the sense of extreme awe and reverence are upon the lips of workmen, carriage-drivers, shoe-blacks, and others of more exalted occupations. Every little offense is accompanied by a religious oath of some kind. In a hotel-parlor we asked a respectable-looking gentleman how he liked the new president-elect (Cleveland), and his emphatic answer was strongly Hebraic. "By G—" he said, "I tell you he is a devil." The gentleman was afterward known to be a staunch Republican. We started in an emigrant train toward the East, and when the car stopped with a jerk so that we were almost thrown out of our seats, one of our fellow-passengers expressed his vexations with another Hebraism, "J——Ch——," and accompanied it with a stamping. And so forth. All these were of course utterly strange to our ears. Soon I was able to discover the deep profanity that lay at the bottom of all these Hebraisms, and I took them as open violations of the Third Commandment, of whose special use and significance I had never been able to comprehend thus far, but now for the first time, was taught with "living examples."

So universal is the use of religious terms in every-day speech of the American people, that a story is told of a French immigrant who carried an English-French dictionary in his pocket, to which he referred for every English word that he heard from the very beginning of his departure from Havre. On his landing at the Philadelphia wharf, the commonest word that he heard the people spoke was "damn-devil." He at once went to his dictionary, but failing to find such a word therein, he threw it away, thinking that a dictionary that did not contain so common a word must be of no further use to him in America.

The report that money was the almighty power in America was corroborated by many of our actual experiences. Immediately after our arrival at San Francisco, our faith in "Christian civilization" was severely tested by a disaster that befell one of our numbers. He was *pick-pocketed* of a purse that contained a five-dollar-gold piece! "Pick-pocket-ing in Christendom as in Pagandom," we cautioned to each other; and while in dismay and confusion we were consoling our robbed brother, an elderly lady, who afterward told us that she believed in the universal salvation of mankind, good as well as bad, took our misfortune heavily upon her heart, and warned us of further dangers, as pick-pocketing, burglarying, high-way-ing, and all other transgressions of sinful humanity were not unknown in her land as well. We did only wish, however, that that crank who despoiled us of that precious five-dollar-piece would never go to heaven.

But it was when we came to Chicago that mammonism in the highest spiritual sense was revealed to our vision. In the depot-restaurant, where, after four-days' jerking in an emigrant train, we refreshed ourselves with a piece each of cold chicken, with grateful remembrance of the Refresher of our souls, we were surrounded by a group of waiters whose black skin and wooly hair were the unmistakable signs of their Hamitic origin. On our bowing our heads before we partook of the gifts of the table, one of them patted our shoulders, and said, "you're gut men, you!" Upon our telling them of our faith (we believed in the literal sense of Matt. 10: 32), they told us that they were all Methodists, and took a great

deal of interest in the universal spreading of God's
Kingdom. Soon there appeared another Hamite,
who was introduced to us as the deacon of their
church. He was very kind to us, heard with seeming interest what we told him of the advance of
our mutual Faith in our land. We exchanged our
good wishes and exhortations for the cause of our
common Lord and Master. He attended upon us
for full two hours, when the time for our departure came. He took all our valises upon his
shoulders, followed us to the place where our
tickets were examined—such was his care and attention for us. With courtesy and many thanks
we extended our hands to take our goods to ourselves, to which our Methodist deacon objected;
but stretching forth his dusky hand toward us,
said, "Jist gib me somding." He had our valises
in his custody, and only "somding" could recover
them from his hands. The engine-bell was ringing; it was not time to argue with him. Each of
us dropped a 50-cent piece into his hand, our
things were transferred to us, to a coach we hastened, and as the train began to move, we looked
to each other in amazement, and said, "Even
charity is bartered here." Since then we never
have trusted in the kind words of black deacons.

One year after this, when I was again robbed
of my new silk-umbrella on a Fall River steamer,
—whose superb ornamentation and exquisite
music conveyed to me no idea whatever of the
spirit of knavery that lurked underneath,—and so
did once more liberate my heathen innocence, I
felt the misfortune so keenly, that only once in
my life I prayed for the damnation of that ex-
ecrable devil, who could steal a shelter from a
homeless stranger at the time of his dire necessity. Even the Chinese civilization of forty cen-

turies ago could boast of a state of society when nobody picked up things dropped on the street. But here upon Christian waters, in a floating palace, under the spell of the music of Handel and Mendelssohn, things were as unsafe as in a den of robbers.

Indeed, insecurity of things in Christendom is something to which we were wholly unaccustomed. Never have I seen more extensive use of keys than among these Christian people. We in our heathen homes have but very little recourse to keys. Our houses, most of them, are open to everybody. Cats come in and out at their own sweet pleasures, and men go to siesta in their beds with zephyrs blowing over their faces; and no apprehensions are felt of our servants or neighbors ever transgressing upon our possessions. But things are quite otherwise in Christendom. Not only are safes and trunks locked, but doors and windows of all descriptions, chests, drawers, iceboxes, sugar-vases, all. The housewife goes about her business with a bundle of keys jingling at her side; and a bachelor coming home in the evening has first to thrust his hand into his pocket to draw out a cluster of some twenty or thirty keys to find out one which will open to him his lonely cell. The house is locked from the front-door to the pin-box, as if the spirit of robbery pervaded every cubic-inch of the air. In our country we have this saying, uttered by the most suspicious of mankind, I suppose: "When you look at a light, think that it is a fire which can consume all your substances; when you look at a man, think that he is a robber who can rob you of all your possessions." But never have I seen this injunction put into practice in a more literal sense than in a well-locked American household. It is a

miniature feudal castle modified to meet the prevailing cupidity of the age. Whether a civilization which requires cemented cellars and stone-
cut vaults, watched over by bull-dogs and battal-
ions of policemen, could be called Christian is
seriously doubted by honest heathens.

In no other respect, however, did Christendom
appear to me more like heathendom than in a
strong race prejudice still existing among its people. After a "century of dishonor," the copper-
colored children of the forest from whom the land
was wrested by many cruel and inhuman means,
are still looked upon by the commonality as no
better than buffaloes or Rocky Mountain sheep, to
be trapped and hunted like wild beasts. As for
ten millions of Hamites whom they originally imported from Africa, as they now import Devon
bulls and Jersey cows, and just for the very same
purpose, there was shown considerable sympathy
and Christian brothership some thirty years ago;
and beginning with John Brown, that righteous
Saxon, 500,000 of the flower of the nation were to
be butchered to atone for the iniquity of merchan-
dising upon God's images. And though they now
have so condescended themselves as to ride in the
same cars with the "darkies," they still keep up
their Japhetic vanity by keeping themselves at
respectable distances from the race which they
bought with their own blood. Down in the state
of Delaware, whither I was once taken by a friend
of mine as his guest, I was astonished to find a
separate portion of a town given up wholly to ne-
groes. Upon telling my friend that this making
a sharp racial distinction appeared to me very Pa-
gan-like, his emphatic answer was that he would
rather be a Pagan and live separate from "nig-

gers," than be a Christian and live in the same
quarters with them!

But strong and unchristian as their feeling is
against the Indians and the Africans, the prejudice, the aversion, the repugnance, which they en-
tertain against the children of Sinim is something
which we in heathendom have never seen the like.
The land which sends over missionaries to China,
to convert her sons and daughters to Christianity
from the nonsense of Confucius and the superstitions of Buddha,—the very same land abhors even
the shadow of a Chinaman cast upon its soil.
There never was seen such an anomaly upon the
face of this earth. Is Christian mission a child's
play, a chivalry more puerile than that engaged
the wit of Cervantes, that it should be sent to a
people so much disliked by the people who send it?

The main reasons which make the Chinese so
objectionable to the Christian Americans I understand to be three:

1. *The Chinese carry away all their savings to
their home, and thus impoverish the land.*—That
is, that they might be acceptable to the Americans, they must spend up all they earned in America, and go home empty-handed. A strange doctrine this to hear from the people who inculcate
the lessons of industry and provision upon themselves. "All things whatsoever ye would that
men should do to you, do ye even so to them." Do
all the American and European merchants and
savants and engineers who come to *our* shores,—
do *they* leave all their earnings with us, and go
home without bank-accounts in their favor? Do
we not pay each one of them, 200, 300, 400, 500,
800 dollars a month in solid gold, scarcely a third
of which he usually spends in our land, and goes
away with the rest to buy ease and comforts in

his homeland? And yet *we* send them out with thanks, with presents of silk-robes and bronze-vases, and oftentimes with imperial decorations and pensions affixed thereto. They did the service corresponding to the money we paid them (at least we suppose they did), and we do not think ourselves robbed by them. By what laws under \ heaven are the Chinese compelled to leave all their earnings in America after they have helped to cut a railroad through the Rocky Mountains, and planted and watered vineyards in California? They do not carry away gold for nothing, as self-styled Christians sometimes did by directing muzzles of guns at the defenceless heathens, and kidnapping supple babies from the breasts of suckling mothers. The Chinamen leave the work behind them equivalent to the money they carry away. The gold is not theirs by Nature's inherent law, and who art thou that deniest the sacred right of property to the sons of honest toil? *We* the "pitiable heathens" send our foreign employes with honors and ceremonies, and they the "blessed Christians" kick us out with derisive languages. Can these things be, O God of Vengeance!

2. *These Chinese, with their stubborn adherence to their national ways and customs, bring indecencies upon the Christian community.* —True, pigtails and flowing pantaloons are not very decent things to be seen in the streets of Boston or New York. But do you think corsets and compressed abdomens are fine things to see in the streets of Peking or Hankow? "But Chinese are filthy in their habits, and tricky in their dealings with others," you say. I wish I could show you some specimens of the noble Caucasian race roaming in the Eastern ports, who are as filthy, as

stinky, as putrefactive, as a poor pox-stricken Chinaman who is dungeoned by the San Francisco quarantine in a manner as if he had upset ten imperial thrones. As for the alleged moral obliquity of the Chinese: Have you ever heard of a Chinaman throwing a bombshell at city police, or disgracing the American womanhood in the mid-day sun? Why not enact anti-German laws and anti-Italian laws as well if the social order and decency are your aim? What are the iniquities of the poor Chinamen that you persecute them with so much rigor, except they be their defencelessness and abject submission to your Gothic will? Would that the iniquities of the Caucasian sojourners in our land were counted that they might be weighed over against those of Chinamen! If we had done to American or English citizens in our land half as much indignities as are done to the helpless Chinese in America, we would soon be visited with fleets of gunboats, and in the name of justice and humanity, would be compelled to pay $50,000 per capita for the lives of those worthless loafers, whose only worth as human beings consist in their having blue eyes and white skins, and in nothing more. Christendom seems to possess another Gospel, in addition to one preached by Paul and Cephas, which teaches among other detestable things this:

Might is Right, and Money is that Might.

3. The Chinese by their low wages do injury to the American laborer. — This sounds more plausible than the other two reasons. It is "Protection" applied to the imported labor. I do not like to see any American household deprived of its chicken-pies on Sunday that a Chinaman might have a morsel more of his steamed rice. But let

America's national conscience ask this question
of itself: Is 4,000,000 square miles of land flowing with milk and honey not wide enough for 65,-
000,000 of its people? Are there no spaces left in
Idaho, Montana, and elsewhere, where the packed
population of Canton and Foochow may be given
opportunities of coping with buffaloes and grizzly
bears to subdue the land for humankind?
Where in God's Sacred Writings, or in Nature's
fossiled tablets, can be found a statement that
goes to prove an assumption that America must
be possessed by the white race alone? Or if you
like to be argued with without having your vanity
touched in any way, you may be persuaded thus:
Grudge to the poor Chinamen so much charity as
the unpardoning Jews did to the heathen Gibeon-
ites; that is, make them "hewers of wood and
drawers of water" to you, and you go to some
more lordly occupations befitting your Teutonic
or Celtic origin. Let them wash all your cuffs
and collars and shirts for you; and they will serve
you with lamblike meekness, and for half the
price your own Caucasian laundrymen charge
you. Or send them down into the Arizona or
New Mexico mines to fetch from the bosom of infernal darkness the metal we prize so highly in
day-light. A "strike" is yet unknown among the
poor heathens, unless some of you teach them
how to do it. A class of laborers so meek, so un-
complaining, so industrious, and so cheap, you
cannot find anywhere else under the sun.* That

* "I will admit that at one time I had fears of the Chi-
ese overrunning this country, but for some years I have
had none. * * * I do not know what we would do
without them, and I undertake to say that they are the
most quiet, industrious and altogether commendable class
of foreigners who come here. There is no other class so
quick to learn and none so faithful."—Senator Stanford
of California.

to so use them in a sphere of industry peculiarly their own is not only befitting your Christian profession, but profitable as well for your pockets, you have proved more than once by "smugglings of Chinamen" often enacted upon the Canadian frontiers. Why refuse to bless your fellowmen by "policies" out of jealousies and rum-shops born? Why not believe in the Law of Prophets, and be kind and merciful to strangers, that the Lord of hosts may open you the windows of heaven, and pour you out a blessing, that there shall not be room enough to receive it? But as they now are, the whole tenor of anti-Chinese laws appears to me to be anti-Biblical, anti-Christian, anti-evangelical, and anti-humanitarian. Even the nonsense of Confucius teaches us very much better things than these.

It is perhaps hardly necessary for me to say that I am not a Chinaman myself. Though I am never ashamed of my racial relationship to that most ancient of nations,—that nation that gave Mencius and Confucius to the world, and invented the mariner's compass and printing machines centuries before the Europeans even dreamed of them,—yet to receive in my person all the indignities and asperities with which the poor coolies from Canton are goaded by the American populace, required nothing less than Christian forbearance to keep my head and heart in right order. Here again, American Hebraisms, which are applied even in the nomenclatures of horses, are made use of in the designations of the Chinese. They are all called "John," and even the kind policemen of the city of New York call us by that name. "Pick up those Chinamen in," was the polite language of a Chicago coachman, to whom we paid the regular fare, and did nothing to hurt his vanity as a *protege* of St. Patrick. A well-clad

gentleman sharing the same seat with me in a
car asked me to have my comb to brush his grizzly
beard; and instead of a thank which we in heathendom consider as appropriate upon such an
occasion, he returned the comb, saying, "Well,
John, where do you keep your laundry shop?" An
intelligent-looking gentleman asked us when we
did cut our cues; and when told that we never
had cues, "Why," he said, "I thought all Chinamen have cues." That these very gentlemen, who
seem to take peculiar delight in deriding our Mon-
golian origin, are themselves peculiarly sensitive
as to their Saxon birthright, is well illustrated by
the following little incident:

A group of young Japanese engineers went to
examine the Brooklyn Bridge. When under the
pier, the structure and tension of each of the sus-
pending ropes were being discussed upon, a silk-
hatted, spectacled, and decently dressed American gentleman approached them. "Well, John,"
he intruded upon the Japanese scientists, "these
things must look awful strange to you from
China, ey?" One among the Japanese retorted
the insulting question, and said, "So they must
be to you from Ireland." The gentleman got angry and said, "No, indeed not. I am not Irish."
"And so we are not Chinese," was the gentle re-
joinder. It was a good blow, and the silk-hatted
sulked away. He did not like to be called an
Irish.

Time fails me to speak of other unchristian feat-
ures of Christendom. What about legalized lottery which can depend for its stability upon its
millions in gold and silver, right in face of simple
morality clear even to the understanding of a
child; of widespread gambling propensities, as
witnessed in scenes of cock-fights, horse-race, and

foot-ball matches; of pugilism, more inhuman
than Spanish bull-fights; of lynching, fitted more
for Hottentots than for the people of a free Re-
public; of rum-traffic, whose magnitude can find
no parallel in the trade of the whole world; of
demagogism in politics; of denominational jealousies in religion; of capitalists' tyranny and laborers' insolence; of millionaires' fooleries; of
men's hypocritical love toward their wives; etc.,
etc., etc.? Is this the civilization we were taught
by missionaries to accept as an evidence of the
superiority of Christian Religion over other religions? With what shamefacedness did they de-
clare unto us that the religion which made Europe
and America must surely be the religion from on
high? If it was Christianity that made the so-
called Christendom of to-day, let Heaven's eternal
curse rest upon it! Peace is the last thing we can
find in Christendom. Turmoils, complexities, in-
sane asylums, penitentiaries, poor-houses!

O for the rest of the Morning Land, the quie-
tude of the Lotus Pond! Not the steam whistle
that alarms us from our disturbed sleep, but the
carol of the Bird of Paradise that wakens us from
our delicious slumber; not the dust and jar of an
elevated railroad, but a palanquin borne by a low-
ing cow; not marble mansions built with price of
blood earned in the Wall Street battle-market,
but thatched roofs with sweet contentment in Nature's bounties. Are not sun, moon, and stars
purer and more beautiful objects of worship than
money and honors and empty shows?

O heaven, I am undone! I was deceived! I
gave up what was really Peace for that which is
no Peace! To go back to my old faith I am now
too overgrown; to acquiesce in my new faith is
impossible. O for Blessed Ignorance that might

have kept me from the knowledge of faith other
than that which satisfied my good grandma! It
made her industrious, patient, true; and not a
compunction clouded her face as she drew her last
breath. Hers was Peace and mine is Doubt; and
woe is me that I called her an idolator, and pitied
her superstition, and prayed for her soul, when
I myself had launched upon an unfathomable
abyss, tossed with fear and sin and doubt. One
thing I shall never do in future: I shall never
defend Christianity upon its being the religion of
Europe and America. An "external evidence" of
this nature is not only weak, but actually vicious
in its general effects. The religion that can support an immortal soul must have surer and profounder bases than such a "show" evidence to rest
upon. Yet I once built my faith upon a straw like
that.

CHAPTER VII.

IN CHRISTENDOM.—AMONG PHILANTHROPISTS.

It was well said by a Chinese sage that "he who stays in a mountain knows not the mountain." The fact is, distance lends not only enchantment to a view, but comprehensiveness as well. A mountain in its true proportion can be viewed only from a distance.

So with one's own country. As long as he lives *in* it, he really knows it not. That he may understand its true situation as a part of the great whole, its goodness and badness, its strength and weakness, he must stand away from it. Who is more ignorant of the city of New York than some of its domiciled denizens, to whom the Central Park is the only "wild" in the universe, and the City Museum the hole through which they can peep into the wide world! The English aristocrats are famous for their ignorance about their own Island Empire, which makes their expensive travels around the world almost a necessity to make them anything near sensible subjects of her Britannic Majesty. So oftentimes, missionaries sent out to convert heathens come home converted themselves, not indeed from their Christianity, but from much, very much, of views they used to hold about themselves, Christendom, the "election" of Christians, the damnation of heathens, etc., etc. "Send your darling son to travel," is a saying common among my countrymen. Nothing disenchants a man so much as traveling.

My views about my native land were extremely one-sided while I stayed in it. While yet a heathen, my country was to me the centre of the universe, the envy of the world. "The soil gives the five grains* in luxurious abundance; its climate the equablest in the world; its scenery the richest, its seas and lakes like the eyes of a maiden, and its pine-clad hills her crescent-shaped eyebrows; the land itself overcharged with spirit, the very abode of gods, the fountain of light." Such, I say, I thought my country to be, while I was yet a heathen. But how opposite when I was "converted!" I was told of "happy lands far, far away;" of America, with four hundred colleges and universities; of England, the Puritan's home; of Germany, Luther's Fatherland; of Switzerland, Zwingli's pride; of Knox's Scotland and Adolphus' Sweden. Soon an idea caught my mind that my country was really "good-for-nothing." It was a heathen land which required missionaries from other countries to make it good. God of Heaven had never thought much about it; He left it so many years wholly in the hand of devils. Speaking of any of its moral or social defects, we were constantly told that it was no so in America or Europe. Whether it could ever be a Massachusetts or an England, I sincerely doubted. I did truly believe that the world would not be any worse even if my country were wiped out of existence. "Is there such a thing as tax-paying in Japan?" a girl in a mission school was heard to have asked her teacher. Poor, innocent soul, she imagined her own people to be in such a degradation that extortion or some other heathen method of "sipping the people's blood" was still re-

* Rice, wheat, barley, bean, millet.

sorted to in her land, and equity and right the things peculiar to her adored America. "Denationalizing influences of missionaries" are *not* phenomèna wholly unknown in mission-fields.

But looking at a distance from the land of my exile, my country ceased to me a "good-for-nothing." It began to appear superbly beautiful,— not the grotesque beauty of my heathen days, but the harmonic beauty of true proportions, occupying a definite space in the universe with its own historic individualities. Its existence as a nation was decreed by Heaven Itself, and its mission to the world and human race was, and is being, distinctly announced. It was seen to be a sacred reality, with purpose high and ambition noble, to be for the world and mankind. Thrice thankful was I that such a glorious view of my country was vouchsafed to my vision.

This is not the only salubrious result of foreign travel, however. Under no other circumstances are we driven more into ourselves than when we live in a strange land. Paradoxical though it may seem, we go into the world that we may learn more about ourselves. Self is revealed to us nowhere more clearly than where we come in contact with other peoples and other countries. Introspection begins when another world is presented to our view.

Several things conspire to bring about this result. First and most evident of all, loneliness is unavoidable to any sojourner in a strange land. With the best of friendship he may form in it, and the freest use of its language, he is still a stranger. A conversation, which otherwise might have been enjoyable and exhilarating, is made burdensome by an extra mental energy required in conjugating verbs for right tenses and moods, in giving

singular predicates to singular nouns, (things unknown in my language), and in selecting right
prepositions out of scores that differ but slightly
from one another. Invitations to friendly dinners
are deprived of much of the anticipated pleasures
on account of extra attentions necessary for conducting prehensions, mastications, and deglati-
tions in accordance with the fixed table-laws. We
would greatly prefer, therefore, to be alone, and
help ourselves in our own styles, undisturbed by
the staring looks of some ladies watching our savage demeanors with their keen, critical eyes.
Loneliness becomes doubly sweet to us under
such circumstances. Monologues and introspec-
tions are daily feasted upon, and the objective
and the subjective selfs are in constant communion with each other.

Secondly, one is more than an individual when
he steps out of his country. He carries in himself
his nation and his race. His words and actions
are judged not simply as his, but as his race's and
his nation's as well. Thus in a sense, every sojourner in a strange land is a minister plenipoten-
tiary of his country. He represents his land and
his people. The world reads his nation through
him. We know that nothing steadies a man so
much as the sense of high responsibility. And
when I know that my country is condemned or ap-
plauded as I behave myself meanly or nobly, then
flippancies, flirtings, and levities of all sorts de-
part from me at once. I become as grave as an
ambassador to the sublime court of St. James.
Hence reflection, consideration, and judgment.
He who behaves otherwise is not worthy of his nation, I believe.

Thirdly, we all know what homesickness is. It
is Nature's recoil upon one's uncongenial sur-

roundings.   Those familiar faces and hills and
fields, which we now miss, but cannot erase from
our mental vision, seek for dominancy in our
souls; and in our very efforts to conform ourselves to the new environments, the home with its
jealous love binds us more to its sweet recollections.   Then comes Melancholy to dissolve the
aching heart to tears, and drives us into dells and
woods to engage in musings and fitful prayers.
Our eyes follow the sun as he rolls down into the
western main, and bid him to tell our dear ones
at home as they behold him in his rising glory,
that we are well here and think of them.   Thus
in spirits' land we dwell.   Swallows come and go,
men sell and gain or lose, but to the exiled from
home monotony runs throughout the year,—communion with himself, with God, and with spirits.

It must have been with some such providential
purposes that Moses was driven to the land of the
Midianites before he came forth as a deliverer of
his people.   Elijah's "flight to Beer-sheba" has
ever been a fact of infinite consolation to one who
in a strange land strives to seek God in the loneliness of his soul.

"Sit on the desert stone
Like Elijah at Horeb's cave alone;
And a gentle voice comes through the wild,
Like a father consoling his fretful child,
That banishes bitterness, wrath, and fear,
Saying 'Man is distant, but God is near.'"

St. Paul's "Arabia" has always been construed in
such a sense, for nothing could be more natural
than that the Apostle to the Gentiles should have
his term of internal discipline, that he might
grasp the Son "at the first hand," and come forth
and announce to the world and say:—

"I certify you, brethren, that the gospel which

was preached of me is not after man. For I
neither received it of man, neither was I taught
it, but by the revelation of Jesus Christ."

Soon after my arrival in America, I was "picked
up" by a Pennsylvania doctor, himself a philanthropist of the most practical type. After prob-
ing a little into my inner nature, he agreed to take
me into his custody, and placed me among his "attendants" with a prospect that I might taste all
the ways up from the very lowest of practical
charity. The change was quite a sudden one for
me from an officer in an Imperial Government to
an attendant in an asylum for idiots; but I did
not feel it, as the Carpenter-Son of Nazareth
taught me now an entirely new view of life.

Let me here note that I entered a hospital service with somewhat the same aim as that which
drove Martin Luther into his Erfurth convent. I
took this step, not because I thought the world
needed my service in that line, much less did I
seek it as an occupation (poor though I was), but
because I thought it to be the only refuge from
"the wrath to come," there to put my flesh in subjection, and to so discipline myself as to reach the
state of inward purity, and thus inherit the kingdom of heaven. At the bottom, therefore, I was
egoistic, and I was to learn through many a painful experience that egoism in whatever form it
appears is of devils, and is sin. In my efforts to
conform myself to the requirements of Philanthropy, which are perfect self-sacrifice and total
self-forgetfulness, my innate selfishness was revealed to me in all its fearful enormities; and
overpowered with the darkness I descried in myself, I sunk, and writhed in unspeakable agonies.
Hence the dreary records of this part of my existence. The present-day reader, more accustomed
to the sunny side of human existence, may not be

disposed to take them in with any degree of seriousness; but to the sufferer himself, they are the accounts of veritable Actualities out of which came the long-sought Peace, and all the blessed fruits resulting therefrom.

But aside from my internal struggles, my life in the Hospital was very far from being unpleasant. The Superintendent was a man who took genuine interest in my welfare, and looked after me with real affections, second only to those he lavished upon his own children. He believed in the right state of body for right morals and conducts; so naturally his solicitude toward me was more about my stomach than about my soul. Those who knew him not took him for a rabid materialist, especially when they heard him talk about his favorite subject, "Moral Imbecility," meaning by that constitutional depravity caused by parental mistakes and vile environments. But a materialist and atheist he was not. He had a firm trust in Providence, as shown in his constant references to it as the Hand that guided him through all his life. He even attributed my coming under his care to Something more than mere chance, and cared and watched over me accordingly. His Biblical knowledge was extensive, and though not strictly "Orthodox" in his religious professions, he abhored the heartless intellectualism, and would often pronounce Unitarianism as "the narrowest and driest of sects," and this, notwithstanding his wife was a charming Unitarian woman, and a large part of his employes were recruited from Massachusetts. He indeed sometimes "roared like a devil," as my Irish colleagues used to tell me, at which the whole house trembled, and everybody tried to stand at a safe distance from him; but withal he had a heart encompassing the whole of his large heterogeneous family, a maimed little Johnny and a mute little Sophie being equally at ease with him as our able and strong matron, who would often keep him at bay, and bid him to keep his mouth shut. The Doctor's musical skill was considerable, and many a time after the family was dismissed, he sung to the piano played by our music teacher; and many a time in my internal agonies, my soul was stilled by his tremulous voice as he threw his whole fervor into his favorite piece.

> "Slowly by God's hand unfurled,
> Down around the weary world,
> Falls the darkness; Oh! how still
> Is the working of His will."

But it was neither his religion nor his music that made me his admirer and faithful learner. It was his systematic thought steadily carried into practice, his well-directed will which gradually subdued rocky Pennsylvania hills, and made out of them a flourishing colony for the most unfortunate of mankind; his administrative skill which could rule and guide and keep in subjection some seven hundred demented souls; his large ambition extending to dim future, which it will take his lifetime, and his sons' lifetime to realize,—all these made him a wonder and a study to me, such that I never have seen either in my homeland or anywhere else. If he helped me not in unriddling the tough religious doubts with which I was then afflicted, he taught me how to make the most out of my life and religion; that Philanthropy with whatever high and delicate sentiment it might be backed, is of but little practical use in this practical world, unless it has a clear head and an iron will to make it a blessing to the suffering humanity. No courses in "Practical Theology" could have taught me this invaluable lesson so well and so impressively as the living example of this practical man. He it was who rescued me from degenerating into that morbid *religiosity* (if I may so call it) wherein those so afflicted

"Sigh for wretchedness, yet shun the wretched,
  Nursing in some delicious solitude,
Their daint loves and slothful sympathies."

The Doctor remained to the last hour the most trusted of my friends; and with all the differences in age, race, nationality and temperament, the love I contracted toward him has proved to be the most enduring. Oft in my New England college days, when others of my good friends were solicitous about my heart and head, he remembered my stomach, and would often send me some substantial helps, bidding me to fetch good square meals and be cheerful. And even after my return home, when my out-of-routine ways of action put my mental and spiritual sanity in question with many who belonged to the same household of Faith with me, it was he who never doubted my Veracity as well as Orthodoxy, and sent me succor and cheer from beyond the ocean. Indeed it was he who *humanized* me. My Christianity would have been a cold and rigid and unpractical thing had I only books and colleges and seminaries to teach me in it. In how manifold a way the Great Spirit does mould us!

Mrs. Superintendent was a Unitarian. In all my readings in Christian literature at home, I conceived anything but favorable opinions about

Unitarianism. I thought it worse than heathenism, and more dangerous because of its seeming affinity to Christianity. I confess, at first I looked upon her with strong suspicions. I imagined she was all brain and no heart, insensible to all that was tender and divinely womanly in the life of the Great Master. And I did not conceal my repugnance of the Unitarian doctrines from before my good hostess,—a rude barbarian as I was. But lo! she proved her possession of heart, a good tender womanly heart, by her *work* in accordance with her own Unitarian principles. My Orthodoxy was no obstacle to her in befriending me. She with the Doctor succored me frequently, and more than he, with her womanly instinct, she "sniffed out" my peculiar pains and comforted me accordingly. Oft during her last illness she remembered me in the tenderest terms; and only a few days before she joined Dorothea Dix and other Unitarian saintesses the one who "incorrigibly" supported the Puritanic doctrines was not forgotten; and as her last mission-work for the heathen, she sent me from beyond the seas a Christmas gift of most substantial shape to help me forward in the work which she knew was not Unitarian. I believe an Orthodoxy that cannot be reconciled with such a Unitarianism is not worthy to be called Orthodox or Straight-Doctrined. The true liberality, as I take it, is allowance and forbearance of all honest beliefs with an unflinching conviction in one's own faith. Belief in myself that I *can* know *some* Truth, and *disbelief* in myself that I can know *all* Truths, are the foundations of the true Christian liberality, the sources of all goodwills and peaceful dealings with all mankind. Of course I was not converted to these healthy views in a day, but that our worthy Mrs. Superintendent

was largely instrumental in bringing me up to
this ideal, I have no doubt whatever.

Another inspiring object in the Hospital was
its matron! No man I know of was firmer than
she; yet she was a woman! She scoured through
the spacious building from one end to the other,
casting her observant eyes on this boy and that
girl; and woe to a careless attendant who put
Johnny's stockings to Georgie's feet, or Sarah's
bonnet upon Susie's head. That woman *can* rule as
well as man was demonstrated to me by this worthy lady beyond any question of doubt. She certainly is a product of Christian America, to whom
heathendom with all the grace and virtue of its
womanhood cannot bring forth any equal.

One more lovable soul to whom I became firmly
attached during my hospital days I must not fail
to mention, as one who smoothed away much of
my angular Christianity. He was from the state
of Delaware, was decidedly a Southerner in sympathy, a skilled young physician, an Episcopalian
in his religious professon, agile and dexterous,
could make an excellent actor, could write poetry,
an admirer of the Stuart kings, good, kind, and a
most sympathetic friend. In his presence, disap-
peared all at once my prejudice against the Rebel-
South, engendered in my bosom by my New England sympathies and acquaintances. My Puritanic faith and Cromwellian admiration were no
obstacles to admit him to my confidence and love.
He once took me to his Delaware home, that he
might show me real ladies, at all comparable to
those whom I described to him as my ideals. He
said that such did really exist in America, but not
in Pennsylvania or Massachusetts. He hired a
hackney coach, and took me round first
to the Governor's house, and then to the

ex-Governor's, and so on; and as often as we came out of the presence of a beauty to whom we paid our homage, he asked me "How is that?" Upon telling him that she was not yet up to my ideal, he tried another, and then still another, doing his utmost to wrest the words of approbation from me, as the old knight did from his contestant for his idol. But I remained true to myself, and disappointed him at last. "What do you want then in Delaware?" he said to me finally in bewilderment. It was the peach season, and I studied in Geography while at home about the superlative quality of Delaware peaches. I therefore asked for some of the best of them in the state. Such he speedily and gladly ordered, and I had all I wanted and was perfectly satisfied.—This was he who revealed to me the half of America from which my Yankee sympathies had kept me in ignorance. Generous, sympathetic, true, unsuspicious,—why the whole of American Christianity does not go by dollars and cents, with Jonathan Edwards and Theodore Parker. There is such a thing as *chivalric Christianity*, a thing very much to my national heart. I took up somewhat of the spirit of my Southern friend, committed to memory many passages from the Book of Common Prayer which he presented me with, and began to take delight in attending the Episcopal services. Led by God's Spirit, breadth does never contradict one's growing conviction in his own faith; and I am ever thankful that I befriended half of Christendom through my Delaware friend, without weakening in the least my unbounded admiration for Oliver Cromwell, and my attachments to those precious truths contained in the Puritanic form of Christianity.

The limited space only forbids me to make men-

tion of other good friends and sweet influences, who and which acted upon me during my stay in the Hospital. Even from the Irish soil, and that not from among its gentries, came inspirations and widening of my mental and spiritual horizons. One strong man I particularly remember, who had a worshipful admiration for Gladstone, and who, when I told him of my envy for his owning such a mighty sovereign as Queen Victoria, signified his strong dissent with a stamping and a remark: "I would rather be ruled by the king of Abyssinia than be a subject of that d—able woman." And yet what a goodness of heart, and piety too, in these misrepresented sons and daughters of the Emerald Isle.

With these descriptions of my surroundings I may be allowed to give some more of my diaries.

Jan. 1, 1885.—Cold. Last night felt much about 'justification by faith! Was on duty during night. The first time I took up the work of caring the sick. I thanked God that He opened a way for me.

The first day as an attendant in an asylum. The long-cherished line of labor, hallowed by the names of John Howard, Elizabeth Fry, and innumerable other saints and saintesses, was now opened to me. Indeed, I felt I became a saint myself. But already from the very beginning of this my attempt to justify myself by "the works of the law," a voice said deep down in my bosom, "a man is justified by faith without the deeds of the law."

Jan. 6.—Read the Book of Job; much consoled.

Again with the help of the venerable Albert Barnes. The two volumes of his Commentaries were hurried through without a stop. That the final outcome of all evils is good, was now indelibly impressed upon my mind. Ever since I seldom have missed this view of life, even amidst the darkest of clouds.

Jan. 11, Sunday.—Was on duty all the day through. Read Havergal; much taught in spiritual things.

Jan. 25, Sunday.—This life is a school where we are taught how to enter the heaven. The greatest achievement of this life, therefore, is to learn "the precious and eternal lessons."

New lessons are being taught by ministering angels, Francis Havergal the most conspicuous among them. Till then this earthly life was all in all to me, even under the Christian dispensation. The new faith was accepted more for utilitarian purposes, such as happy homes, free governments, etc., than for its intrinsic spiritual worth. "To make my country as strong as Europe or America," was the prime aim of my life, and I welcomed Christianity, as I thought it a great engine for carrying out this design. And O how many do still accept it for its socio-political reasons! But now the love of country was to be sacrificed for the love of heaven, that the former might be restored to me in its truest and highest significance.

Feb. 2.—The idea of my sonship to God; greatly encouraged.

Feb. 11.—Read Phillips Brooks on "Influence of Jesus," and greatly encouraged.

A grand discovery that I am 'God's son and not his brother or equal. Why strive to compete with him in strength and purity, that I be received upon "equal footings" by Him? Presumptuous little god of the world! know thyself, and things will go well with thee.

And Phillips Brooks! what struggling souls did he strengthen and support? What a depth under his surplice, and what a broadness behind his Prayer-Book! As I pored over his book, I thought he knew personally all my ills for which he had specifics to offer. A wayfarer takes in a breath after a draught of his elixir, and for a week or two, he marches on with songs upon his lips, the earth with all its bristles and mountains and valleys leveled and smoothed before him.

Feb. 14.—As far as I know is my own knowledge and truth. The world may have different opinions, but they are not mine; hence I am not responsible for them. Let me care for what I know, and for no more.

The extent and limit of my knowledge was to be defined that I might armor myself against the multitudinous opinions which were now forced upon me for acceptance. America is a land of sects, where each tries to augment its numbers at the expense of others. Already such strange isms as Unitarianism, Swedenborgism, Quakerism, etc., to say nothing of others with which I was already familiar, were being tried upon me. The poor heathen convert is at loss which to make his own; so I made up my mind to accept none of them. What mortals under heaven can make a "right choice" out of dozens and scores of denominations, each having its own merits and demerits? Why torment a poor convert with the etymology of βαπτιεω and persuade him to be "dipped," when authorities equally as great and pious maintain that even sprinkling is not necessary for his eternal salvation. Be merciful to the poor convert, ye "Christians at home."

Feb. 18.—Much doubting; not a little troubled. My heart must be fixed upon God. Men's opinions are various, but God's Truth must be one. Unless taught by God Himself, the true knowledge cannot be obtained.

Horrid struggles with the "selections" of Truth. Is Jesus a God or a man? If I believe He is a man, shall I not be condemned in eternal hell-fire? Yet they say that Emerson, Garrison, Lowell, Martineau, and other great and brave and learned men said that He was a man. My belief in the divinity of Christ was then as foolish and groundless as the superstitious idolatary I had left behind with so much sacrifice. While my struggle upon this point is yet unsettled, another set of divines comes to me, and kindly cautions me not to be deceived by Protestant devils, and favors me with a copy of Cardinal Gibbons' "Faith of Our Fathers," to peruse it with all prayerful diligence. And as soon as my attention is seriously turned toward the solution of this momentous problem, the agnostic in the name of Darwin, Huxley, and Spencer, admonishes me to give up the futile question, and to rest in the visible and the tangible. Then souls in all outward appearances as pious as Madame Guiyon herself, tells me that *their* prophet

Swedenborg saw heaven with his own eyes, and testified with all his mighty intellect that all what he said and wrote was absolutely true. But says great physiologist Dr. Flint, that Swedenborg was a genuine lunatic. Woe is a conscientious heathen convert in the midst of all these controversies. His mind is hurled from one end of the intellectual universe to the other, with no position safe from some attacks of most ponderous nature. Once more I thought of peace and serenity in my grandma's "heathen" faith. Say not, O ye sect-bound Christians, "Better one year of Europe than a cycle of Cathay;" for you promised us a peace which you really do not have. If dissensions and religious animosities are the things to be desired, we had them enough in "Cathay" without entangling ourselves in fresh dissensions of your make and origin. I remember I once went to a missionary and asked him the *raison d'etre*, if there was one, of sects among Christians. He told me that in his view the existence of sects was a real blessing, as it engendered "emulation" among different denominations, and thus brought about more purity in churches, and rapider growth of God's kingdom. When, however, a few months after this, we started up a new church of our own, contrived in a fashion not very palatable to his taste, the very same missionary sharply reprimanded our audacity, by telling us that we must not add one more new sect to hundreds which were already disgracing the cause of Christianity. But we never have been able to comprehend his logic. If the existence of sects is "a real blessing," why not increase the number of sects, and get more benefit out of them! But if it is a curse, as we poor converts imagine it to be, why not attempt to annihilate it, and make Methodism,

Presbyterianism, Congregationalism, Quakerism, and all other harmless and harmful isms into one great united whole. Crank-headed as we are, we never can unriddle the paradoxical statement of our missionary friend.

March 8.—Feeling the importance of sanctification more and more. The "Ideal Purity" lies before my eyes, but I cannot enter that state. A wretched being that I am!

March 22.—Man is too finite a creature to be able to rest upon, and occupy, the whole of the Infinite Foundation of Wisdom. The only thing he can do is to lodge himself in a little corner of this Foundation. As soon as he gets to even this corner, he can be calm and quiet,—so strong is the Rock. This explains the existence of different sects, and the success of every one of them.

A more humane and rational explanation of "sects." I believe Phillips Brooks helped me out to this.

April 5, Easter Sunday.—Beautiful day. Spirit was poured out, and for the first time in my life, had a glimpse of Heaven and Immortality! O the joy inestimable! A moment of such holy joy is worth years of all the joys which the world can give. My spiritual blindness was felt more and more, and I prayed earnestly for light.

A day of Resurrection indeed! After months of continual gloom and wrestlings with Spirit, this revelation and respite were welcome to me beyond my powers of description. I remember I tasted the painted eggs placed before me with a relish more than lingual. In them, (i. e. when they were fresh, and not after they were boiled and hardened and painted,) I read a sermon illustrasting the then state of my soul. All my stock of embryological knowledge was now brought before my mind for spiritualization, and I pondered in what stage of soul-development I then was,— whether it was in the "cleavage stage," or in the "mulberry stage," or so far advanced as to be near the "chick stage." Soon the shell shall be broken, and I shall mount high on my wings to my Savior and Perfection. O for more light!

April 6.—More zest and fervor in teaching the idiotic children.

The day before this, I came in contact with one of the most remarkable men I ever have seen in my life-time. The same was the late James B. Richards, of world-wide renown as an indefatigable teacher of idiotic children. I heard from his very lips some of his early pedagogic experiences, demonstrating to us the practical possibility of "showing the Father" even to the lowest of His children. The impression I received was electric, and its effect, permanent. Since then Philanthropy and Education ceased to be the works of mere Pity and Utility. Both were seen to have high religious purposes,—dispencers of God, the only Good. My attendantship in the asylum was now glorified to a holy and sacred office, and Duty dropped all the slavish elements it had in it.

Him, Richards, Unitarian in his church-relation-
ship, I count among the best missionaries that
have been sent to me. His personality, his depth
of sympathy, saying nothing of his extraordinary
genius as a teacher, smoothed away much of my
Trinitarian prejudices I was bred up to in my
Orthodox relationship and reading.

April 8.—The highest conception of human
capabilities may be the origin of Unitarianism in its purest and highest form. Man,
however, cannot attain his highest possible
moral altitude by his own efforts; so he drags
down Christ to suit his weak intellect.

Conception of God is perfectly clear till we
come to Christ. Here all stumble. I often
think how clear a view must I have with regard to my God had there been no Christ.

Christ a stumblingblock, not only to the
heathen Greeks of old, but to the heathen
Japanese, Chinese, and all other heathens
of this very day. The Unitarian explanation of
him is too simple for the mystic Oriental, but the
Trinitarian "theory" is no less unbelievable. Who
shall roll away the stone for me?

April 16.—Read Fernald's "True Christian
Life."

April 18.—Much interested in reading
Drummond's "Natural Law in Spiritual
World."

April 19.—Took great interest in reading Revelation.

Fernald was the first Swedenborgian author I read with any degree of seriousness. Indeed I peeped into "Arcana Celestia" some three years before this, but then it was too spiritual for my materially-disposed mind. But now in a strange land, grappling with great spiritual problems, mysticism of any sort was welcome to me, for what I could not remove in Fact, I could fly over in my Spirit. Then came Drummond to spiritualize my science, and they two made me extremely spiritual. Now there was left nothing that I could not explain away. So I took up Revelation, the book that I had left untouched for fear that it might turn me a skeptic,—a book, I thought, which was intended for angel-kind, and not for inductive human-kind. But if it is a vivid portraiture of man's spiritual experiences, I lacked nothing in me to illustrate every passage in it. The Trinity chasm can also be bridged over in that way, and the Immaculate Conception and Resurrection are soon counted among ofcourses. And that fearful struggle about the reconciliation of Genesis and Geology, the struggle that drove the famed author of the "Natural History of Selbourne" to madness—it too melts away as easily as September frost before the sun, under the treatment of the author of "Arcana Celestia." But I never have counted Swedenborg among blockheads, as many people do. His was a mind beyond my power of conception, and his insights in very many cases are truly wonderful. He who tries to get the whole truth from Swedenborg may stumble; but he that goes to him in true scholarly humility and with Christian reverence, will, I doubt not, come out greatly blessed. After much gross spiritualism into which I sank at my first contact with his doctrines, the influence of that remarkable man upon my thought has ever been healthful. This is not the place, however, to state in detail in what respect it was so.

May 14.—Read Jeremiah; much affected.

May 16.—Jeremiah affected me a great deal.

May 27.—Much benefitted by reading Jeremiah.

My religious readings thus far had been more from "Christian Evidences" and such stuffs, and less from the Bible itself. Hence I conceived an idea that the Old Testament prophesies were mostly future-tellings, delivered unto mankind to astonish the world with "coincidences" when the Savior of the race did come at last. So I early included the books of prophets among the incomprehensible. I read *about* them, but not *in* them. But now with half curiosity and half fear, I peeped into Jeremiah, though the Superintendent once gave us a notice that he would not allow any Jeremiah upon his ground, for such would set the whole house to weeping in sight of all the miseries in the Hospital. And lo! what a book! So human, so understandable; so little of future-tellings in it, and so much of present warnings! Without a single incident of miracle-working in the whole book, the man Jeremiah was presented to me in all the strength and weakness of humanity. "May not all great men be called prophets?" I said to myself. I recounted to myself

all the great men of my own heathen land and
weighed their words and conducts; and I came
to the conclusion that the same God that spoke to
Jeremiah did also speak to some of my own countrymen, though not so audibly as to him; that He
did not leave us entirely without His light and
guidance, but loved us and watched over us these
long centuries as He did the most Christian of
nations. The thought was inspiring beyond my
power of expression. Patriotism that was
quenched somewhat by accepting a faith that was
exotic in origin, now returned to me with hundred-
fold more vigor and impression. I looked at the
map of my country, and weeped and prayed over
it. I compared Russia to Babylonia, and the Czar
to Nebuchadnezzar, and my country to the helpless Judea to be saved only by owning the God of
Righteousness. In my old English Bible I noted
down such remarks as these:

Jer. III, 1-5;—Who can resist this solicitation?

Jer. IV, 1-18;—These are words of sorrow. Ah,
my country, my empire, follow thou not the foot-
steps of Judea.

Jer. IX, 18-31;—Is not Russia of the North our
Chaldea? Etc.

For two years from this time I read almost nothing from my Bible but the Prophets. The whole
of my religious thought was changed thereby.
My friends say that my religion is more a form of
Judaism than the Christianity of Gospels. But
it is not so. I learnt from Christ and His Apostles
how to save my soul, but from the Prophets, *how
to save my country.*

I remained in the hospital service for nearly
eight months, when "doubts" within me became
impossible to be borne for any greater length of
time. Relief must be sought somewhere. The

good Doctor said I needed rest, and prescribed for
me Appolinaris' Water for my torpid liver; for
in his practical view, much, if not all, of so-called
spiritual struggles could be explained by some
derangement of digestive organs. Taking advantage of his medical advice, I went to New
England where I had some friends from my native land, for I thought something "lucky" might
come out by change of locations. My heathen
trust in "good lucks" always cropped out when
I came to extremities.

With a sad heart I left the Hospital and many
good friends I made there, deeply regretting my
imperfect services, and change of plans so soon
after committing myself to the care of the good
Doctor. Philanthropy, "love-man" business, I
found to be not my own till my "love-self" propensity is totally annihilated within me. Soul-
cure must precede body-cure, in my case at least;
and Philanthropy of itself was powerless for the
former purpose.

But be it far from me to say anything de-
preciatory of the work which "angels do envy."
It is a work nobler than which cannot be met with
anywhere else in this wide universe. Some say
mission work to the heathen is nobler. Perhaps
so, since as the body is more than garments, so
the soul is more than *its* garment, the body. But
who ever separated the body from the soul, as
we do the orange-skin from the pulp inside? Who
ever can save the soul without reaching it through
the body? A minister of religion working upon
the depart-in-peace-be-ye-filled-and-warmed principle is as far removed from heaven, as a curer
of the body working upon the health-for-fees principle is near to heaven's opposite extremities.
Philanthropy is Agapanthropy, if you are particu-

lar about the relative meanings of the two Greek words for love. "Medicine" said a Chinese sage, "is an art of love," and as far as I know, the Christianity of Gospels seems to approve this saying though uttered by a heathen. Who then can distinguish Medicine from Theology?

CHAPTER VIII.

IN CHRISTENDOM—NEW ENGLAND COLLEGE LIFE.

I was to see New England by all means, for my Christianity came originally from New England, and she was responsible for all the internal struggles caused thereby. I had a sort of claim upon her, and so I boldly entrusted myself to her. I first went to Boston, and thence to a fishing town near Cape Ann, there to acclimatize myself to New England blue-berries, and to Yankee modes of life and action. For two weeks I wrestled in prayer upon a rocky promontory of the Eastern Massachussetts, with the billows of the Atlantic to moan my wretchedness, and the granite quarries of the state to illustrate the hardness of my heart. I returned to Boston somewhat becalmed. I secluded myself in one of its obscure cow-traced streets about a fortnight more, and then I made my way to the Connecticut valley.

My object in going there was to see a man, the president of a well-known college, of whose piety and learning I had previously tasted in my homeland through some of his writings. To us poor heathens, the idea of great intellectual attainments always carries with it that of imperiousness, and hence of unapproachableness. A man with the double-title of D. D. and LL. D. need not condescend to the commonality to solve its doubts and see to its sorrows. Is not his mind always occupied with "Evolution," "Conservation of

Energy," and such like? To expect from him anything like personal help to my little soul, I thought
to be wholly presumptuous on my part. I was
told, however, that I could see him, and I made
up my mind to see him from a distance, if I could
do nothing else.

Miserably clad in an old nasty suit, with no
more than seven silver dollars in my pocket, and
five volumes of Gibbon's Rome in my valise, I
entered the college town, and soon appeared in
the president's gate. A friend of mine had previously introduced my name to him; so he knew
that a young savage was coming to him. I was
introduced to his parlor, and there waited for my
doom to be stunned by his intellectuality and
Platonic majesty. Hush! he is coming! Prepare
thy soul to stand before his sinless presence. He
may look through thy heart at once, and take thee
for what thou really art, and refuse to own thee
as his pupil. The door opened, and behold the
Meekness! A large well-built figure, the leonine
eyes suffused with tears, the warm grasp of hands
unusually tight, orderly words of welcome and
sympathy,—why, this was not the form, the mind,
the man I had pictured to myself before I saw
him. I at once felt a peculiar ease in myself. I
confided myself to his help which he most gladly
promised. I retired, and from that time on my
Christianity has taken an entirely new direction.

I was given a room in the college dormitory free
of charge; and as I had neither a table, nor a
chair, nor a bed, nor even a washtub, the kind
president ordered the janitor to provide me with
few such necessities. There in a room in the
uppermost story I settled myself, firmly making
up my mind never to move from the place till the
Almighty should show Himself unto me. With

an aim like this in view, I was entirely insensible
to the lack of my personal comforts. The former
occupant of my room had the carpet removed
from the floor, and the new occupant was not able
to re-carpet it. There I found however a table
crippled of its drawers, but as its four feet were
stiff and strong, I made a very good use of it.
There was also an old easy chair with one of its
corners broken off, so that it stood really upon
tripods; but with a slight equiposing of my body,
I could sit and work upon it quite comfortably.
The bedstead was of wooden frame and a good
one, but it squeaked, and the bed-cover harbored
some living specimens of Cimex lectularius, com-
monly called the bed-bug. I provided myself with
a Yankee lamp of the simplest construction, and
this with a small wash-vase besides constituted
the whole of my furnitures. I had my pen and
ink and paper, and a praying heart to fill up all
the rest.

Thus I began my New England college life. To
describe it fully is not demanded by my American
or English readers. I got from it all the fun and
jest which every student carries away with him.
I liked all its professors. Professor in German
was the jolliest man I ever saw. I read Goethe's
Faust with him, and he made it exceedingly interesting to me, adding not a little of his own
pathos to it. The tragedy struck me like a thun-
derbolt from Heaven. I still refer to that "World-
Bible" only less frequently than to the Bible itself.
Professor in History was a genuine gentleman.
He taught me how to be fair in judging the past,
and with it, the present as well. His lectures
were to me a veritable course in Divinity, though
he seldom spoke about religion, but touched mostly upon "the progress of humanity." Professor in

Biblical Interpretation gave me special lessons in Old Testament History and Theism. The good old Doctor looked after me with genuine interest, and as I was the only student in his class, we two had a regular debating club for three terms in succession. He fished out Confucianism and other good heathenisms that were in me, and weighed them over against the Scriptural standards. In Philosophy I was a total failure. My deductive Oriental mind was wholly incompatible with rigorous inductive processes of perceptions, conceptions and all that, all of which appeared to me either as self-evident facts which needed no distinguishing, or as different names for one and the same thing, so treated that the philosopher might have something to do to kill his time. To us Orientals, who depend more upon our sight than upon logic for the establishment of Truth, the Philosophy as I was taught in my New England college is of comparatively little use in clearing up our doubts and spiritual phantasmagorias. I believe no body made a greater mistake than those Unitarian and other intellectually-minded missionaries, who thought that we Orientals are intellectual peoples, and hence we must be intellectually converted to Christianity. We are poets and not scientists, and the labyrinth of syllogism is not the path by which we arrive at the Truth. It is said of the Jews that they came to the knowledge of true God by "a succession of revelations." So I believe all the Asiatics do.

So I liked Geology and Mineralogy more than Philosophy, not only for what they really are, but as helps to lead me to the knowledge of Peace that passeth all understandings. Crystallography was to me a sermon by itself, and the measurement of the angles of a topaz or an amethyst was to me a real spiritual pastime. Then our Professor in these branches of our study was the best of mankind. He could talk on whole hours upon a single stone picked up on the street, while a Roger and a Whitmarsh and other good fellows were indulging in delicious naps in one corner of his lecture-room. I never asked my Professor how he reconciled Genesis to Geology, for I knew his head had no place for such things, stuffed as it was with rocks and minerals and fossils and footprints more than it could easily hold.

But none influenced and changed me more than the worthy President himself. It was enough that he stood up in the chapel, gave out a hymn, read from the Scripture, and prayed. I never have "cut" my chapel-service, i. e. absented myself from it, even for the sole purpose of casting a view upon the venerable man. He believed in God, in the Bible, and in the power of prayer to accomplish all things. I think those innocent fellows who studied their Latin lessons while that holy man prayed will repent of their doings when they go to heaven. To me I needed nothing more than his clear ringing voice to prepare myself for the battle of the day. That God is our Father, who is more zealous of His love over us than we of Him; that His blessings are so emanant throughout the Universe that we need but open our hearts for His fulness to "rush in;" that our real mistakes lay in our very efforts to be pure when none but God Himself could make us pure; that selfishness is really hatred of self, for he that really loves himself should first hate himself and give himself for others; etc., etc.;—these and other precious lessons the good President taught me by his words and deeds. I confess Satan's power over me began to slacken ever since I came in contact with that man. Gradually I was exorcized of my sins original and sins derived. I think after two years of my college life (for I joined the Junior class), I found myself in a path which pointed heavenward. Not that I ceased to stumble, for that I still constantly do, but because I now know that the Lord is merciful, and that He blotted out my sin in His Son, on whom relying I am not estranged from the Everlasting Love. My subsequent diaries will show that such was really the case.

Soon after my settlement in the college, I was taken by the President to attend one of great missionary meetings. Indeed, nothing is more indicative of the christianness of Christendom than these meetings. Heathendom has no such things; for we care nothing about other people's souls. The mere fact that ten thousand intelligent men and women should fill three or four spacious halls to overflowing to hear about how they can make other nations taste the goodness of Gospel, is by itself impressive enough. Granted that many do come to see shows, and that many others come to be such shows, the fact remains clear that to these people the mission work among heathens is worth to be made a show; and it is doubtless the noblest and divinest of all religious shows. But when this Mission-show is partaken by the toughest and coolest of the nation's heads, and men and women deadly earnest about it appear upon the stage, and with scars and wrinkles upon their foreheads, tell of their moral warfare with the Kaffirs and the Hottentotts, then the show ceases to be a show, and we too get fired by it. I advise any one of my non-Christian countrymen to be in one of these Mission-shows whenever he finds such an opportunity in Christendom; and I can assure him that he will not repent of doing so. The show is worth seeing in all respects. He may see in it the reason of Christendom's greatness, and at the same time, that of his country's smallness. He may thus cease to speak loud about "the brutality of Christians." I tell you, those Mission-shows are inspiring.

But the worst lot in these shows falls to some specimens of converted heathens who happen to be there. They are sure to be made good use of, as circus-men make use of tamed rhinoceroses. They are fetched up for shows; and such wonderful shows! Till but recently bowing before wood and stones, but now owning the same God as that of these white people! "O just tell us how you were converted," they clamour; "but in fifteen minutes and no more, as we are going to hear from the great Reverend Doctor So-and-So about the ways and means and rationale of the mission." The tamed rhinoceros is a living illustration; not a blackboard illustration, but the veriest specimen from the veriest field. And those rhinoceroses who like to be seen and petted gladly obey the behest of these people, and in the most awkward manner, tell them how they ceased to be animals and began to live like men. But there are other rhinoceroses who do not like to be so used. They do not like to be robbed of their internal peace by being made shows to the people, all of whom cannot comprehend through what tortuous and painful processes were they made to give up the rhinoceros-life. They like to be left alone, and walk silently in God's green field away from the sight of man. But the circus-men do not usually like such rhinoceroses. So they sometimes bring some wieldy specimens from the Indian jungles for this special purpose, (usually very

young ones), and take them through the land,
show them to the Sunday school children, fetch
them upon pulpits, and make them sing rhinoceros
songs, and get people interested in missionwork
in that way.

Now I, a regenerate rhinoceros, advise the mission circus-men to be more considerate in this
matter. On one hand, they spoil the tamed
rhinoceroses, and also induce the untamed ones to
simulate the tamed, for that they find the easiest
possible way of getting things good for their
rhinoceros-flesh. On the other hand, I believe you
give false conceptions of what the Christian mission really is to the people whom you like to get
interested in your work in that way. I do not
read in the Bible that Paul or Barnabus brought
a Titus or a Timothy to Jerusalem for the purpose
of making them sing Gentile songs, and tell the
brethren there in his queer half-incomprehensible
way " how he cast his idols into fire and clung
unto the Gospel." I read how the great Apostle
defended the cause of Gentiles with all his
vehemence, and told God's people that they were
no better than the godless Gentiles, that both
were condemned in sins, and came short of the
glory of God;—from all which I conclude that to
Paul and Paully-minded people, Gentilism was
nothing to make merry about, or even to be
"pitied," but it was a thing to be sympathized
with, to be taken as their own state, and hence
to be treated with all reverence and Christian
graces. I do not value those contributions raised
by making a Hindoo youth in his native attire
sing Toplady in his own Paoli, any more than I do
money raised by showing tamed ourangoutangs. I
do not call that a Mission-work that appeals to
people's Pharisaic pride, and showing them that

they are better than heathens, urges "the Christians at home" to "pity them." The best of mis-y sionaries are always upholders of the cause and dignity of the people to whom they are sent, and they are as sensitive as the patriotic natives themselves to expose the idolatories and other degradations before the so-called Christian public.

Indeed, there are some people who seem to imagine that the cause of Missions can be upheld only by picturing the darkness of heathens in contrast with the light of Christians. So they make a diagram showing heathens by jet-black squares, and Protestant Christians by white squares. Missionary Magazines, Reviews, Heralds, all are full of the accounts of the wickedness, the degrations, the gross superstitions of heathens, and scarcely any account of their nobleness, godliness, and highly Christlike characters makes its way into their columns. Many a time in our own experiences, we were not a little chagrined to meet no words of approbation for the talks we gave in some mission gatherings, as we touched more upon the virtuous part of our national character, and less upon the heathenish aspect of the same. They said, "If your people are so fine a set of people, why, there is no need of sending them missionaries." "My dear friend," we often replied, "it is those virtuous set of people who hunger after Christianity more than any other class." The fact is, if we heathens are but slightly better than gibbons or chimpanzees, the Christians may give up their mission works as total failures. It is because we know something about Right and Wrong, Truth and Falsehood, that we are readily brought to the Cross of Christ. I sincerely believe that the Christian mission based upon no higher motive than "pity for heathens" may have its support entirely withdrawn, without much detriment either to the sender or to the sent.

March 1.—When God giveth us gifts, they are substantial. Not mere speculations supported by the opinions of others, nor mere visions which are products of imaginations, but real substance which cannot be disturbed by the winds of the world.

March 8.—Very important day in my life. Never was the atoning power of Christ more clearly revealed to me than it is to-day. In the crucifixion of the Son of God lies the solution of all the difficulties that buffeted my mind thus far. Christ paying all my debts, can bring me back to the purity and innocence of the first man before the Fall. Now I am God's child, and my duty is to believe Jesus. For *His* sake, God will give me all I want. He will use me for His glory, and will save me in Heaven at last. * * * * *

Those of you who are "Philosophically" inclined may read the above passage with a sort of pity, if not with disdain. You say, by the advent of new science into this world, the religion of Luther, Cromwell, and Bunyan, has now passed into a "tradition." You say that "it stands against reason" that faith in a dead Saviour should give a man life. I do not argue with you then. Perhaps a thing like "the responsible soul before the Almighty God" has never troubled you much.

Your ambition may not extend beyond this short span of existence called Life, and your Almighty Judge may be that conventional thing called Society, whose "good enough" may give you all the peace you need. Yes, the crucified Saviour is necessary only to him or her who has eternity to hope for, and the Spirit of the Universe to judge his or her inmost heart. To such the religion of Luther and Cromwell and Bunyan is *not* a tradition, but the verity of all verities.

With all the ups and downs that followed the final grasping of the Crucified Son of God, I will not trouble my reader. Downs there were; but they were less than ups. The One Thing rivetted my attention, and my whole soul was possessed by It. I thought of it day and night. Even while bringing up scuttles of coal from the basement-floor to the topmost story where my lodging was, I meditated upon Christ, the Bible, the Trinity, the Resurrection, and other kindred subjects. Once I laid down my two scuttles (I carried two to balance myself) when I reached the middle floor, and then and there burst into a thanks-giving prayer for a new explanation of the Trinity that was revealed to me on my way from the "coal-hill." My paradise came when the vacation be-gan, and the boys all went home to see their mammas, leaving me the sole occupant of the col-lege-hill, to be alone with *my* Mamma, the gentle Spirit of God. The hill that rang with class-yells and other heathenish noises was now transformed into a veritable Zion. Whenever Satan left me free to myself, I pictured to myself the dear and blessed homeland away beyond the seas, and spotted it with churches and Christian colleges, which of course had their existences in my imagi-nations only. No inspiring thought ever came to my mind but I reserved it as a message to my countrymen. Indeed, an empire and its people swallowed up all my leisure hours.

May 26.—Much impressed by the thought that there is so much more good in this world than the evil. Birds, flowers, sun, air,—how beautiful, bright, balmy! Yet man is complaining all the while of the evil. The world needs but one thing to make it a paradise, and that is the Religion of Jesus Christ.

Am getting to be a real optimist, and this just after I passed a severe New England winter without a stove of mine to warm me, and while I was yet in uncertainty as to the payment of my term-bills!

June 3.—Studied the doctrine of Predestination, and was strongly impressed with its import. Heart leaped with joy. Temptations seem to vanish away, and all the noble qualities of my mind burn with emotions. Where is fear, where is the power of the tempter, if I am one of God's chosen elects, predestinated for his heirship before the foundation of the world!

The doctrine that once proved to be the greatest stumbling block to me is now turned to be the corner-stone of my faith. And I believe this doctrine was enunciated for such very purposes. I believe those are pretty sure to find themselves among the elect who are really seriously anxious about their election while they are doing their best to please their God. The non-elect do not usually trouble themselves with this question.

June 5.—O a thought which should humble every Christian! What worthiness attaches to me that I should be one of the elects! Yet to think that I am daily committing sins!

"Enviable delusion!" my Philosopher-friend will say. But not so enviable as you imagine, for the lot of God's elect is the miserablest upon this earth, and you will surely decline it were it offered unto you. *Die-to-self-ing* day-by-day, that is the election. How do you like it, my Philosopher-friend?

June 15.—Salvation of my soul is entirely unconnected with the conditions of my surroundings and worldly fortunes. Even though I be "steeped" in gold, my soul would remain wholly unaffected. Even though I pass through the severest disciplines of an ascetic, my soul would be like a hungry beast, and would pride itself in its devotion. Unless the Spirit of God touches my heart directly, there cannot be any conversion. What a consoling thought! I mourn for poverty, because my flesh suffers thereby. I fear prosperity, because my soul's salvation is in danger. But no! salvation is of God, and no man or thing or circumstance can take it from me. It is surer than a mountain itself.

This is my version of Rom. VIII, 38, 39. Be not

cast down O Poor, for His grace is sufficient unto thee. Be not afraid, O Rich, for He *can* let go a camel through the eye of a needle.

July 31.—A terrific thunder-storm last night. I was just then meditating upon eternal life, and fighting against some of my infirmities. All at once, flashings and thunderings removed these "fleshy elements" from my heart, and I found myself dreaming of being struck by a thunder-bolt and lying in restful peace. The first time in my life when I enjoyed a rattling thunder-storm.

I disliked thunder, and I always thought my end did come when it rattled right above my head. In my heathen days, I called in the help of all my protecting gods, burnt incense to them, and took my refuge under a mosquito-net as the safest place to flee from "the wrath of heaven." And oft in my Christian days as well, my faith was put to the severest test when "God roared" in the cloud. But now by the grace of God, I was thunderproof, for fear of all sorts had departed from my heart by the revelation of the crucified Jesus unto me. I said in my heart, "Strike O Thunder, for I am safe."

Aug. 16.—O what joys and peace in Jesus, joys in loneliness, joys in friendlessness, yea joys too in sinfulness. O my soul, cling to this precious truth, and turn thy whole attention to it!

"A mere rhetorical contrast," my critic will say.

But not so, my friend in Syntax. We Christians do rejoice in our sinfulness. It was the philosopher Leibnitz who said that nothing served to lift mankind more than its fall in Adam. Sin is a lever by which we mount to God through His Son, oftentimes to a height wholly unattainable by men and women of the Marcus Aurelius type.

Sept. 13.—Evening was serene and beautiful. Just when I was going out to my supper, thought came to me that devils cannot attack me when I am dead to the flesh. And this "death to sin" can be accomplished, not by looking into my sinful heart, but by looking up to Jesus crucified. I can be more than a conqueror through Him that loved me. The thought was extremely refreshing, and all the burdens of the day were entirely forgotten. Gratitude filled my heart, and I wished to commemorate the day by partaking the Lord's supper. So I pressed a little juice out of a cluster of wild grapes, and put it in a little porcelain dish. Also I cut a small piece of biscuit. I placed these upon a cleanly-washed handkerchief, and I sat in front of them. After a thanksgiving and a prayer, I took the Lord's body and blood with very thankful heart. Extremely sanctifying. I must repeat this again and again during my life.

"Sacrilegious! Playing with a holy ordinance," the Churchism and other Popish isms will say to this. But why defy the Roman Pope and his fellow priests in this matter of the Sacrament, and grudge to us the same mortals as yourselves this priviledge of remembering the Lord's death when we feel most to do so. If the Pope has no exclusive authority of sanctifying this ceremony, and his vicarship a mere figment of imagination, what authorities have you to support your "apostolicity?" I know a Japanese who presented himself for membership to a certain evangelical church as a baptized Christian, and who, when asked what authorized prelate baptized him, answered "Heaven." The fact was, one summer afternoon, he was deeply convinced of his sin and found forgiveness in crucified Jesus. He thought the occasion was too solemn to let go without presenting himself for the Holy Baptism. But no "licensed minister" was to be found within twenty-five miles of his residence. Just then, however, a summer shower of the most refreshing sort came pouring upon his district. He thought the heaven itself was inviting him to the holy ceremony. So he rushed right into the midst of rain, and there in a reverential attitude had his whole body drenched by the "heavenly water." He felt the process satisfactory to his conscience, and ever since confessed himself as a disciple of Christ before his idolatrous countrymen. I do not disturb other peoples in their reverence toward the host and golden chalices; and I do not wish myself to be disturbed in my preference in these matters. The pith of the whole affair is He Himself, and men do differ in their ways of appropriating Him. Liberty in non-essentials!

Nov. 24.—Thanksgiving Recess begins. A very refreshing rest.—In morning as I got up,

I found outside the door of my room a pile
of ruddy palatable apples in an artistic tri-
angular basket. It was a great surprise to
me. Some kind friend must have left it there
to console my lonely soul. O what a kindness! Remember, my Soul, such an experience! Often a deed of such kind, though small
it is, touches a human heart more than gifts
of hundreds of dollars. How I felt comforted
throughout the whole day, knowing that there
are some unknown souls who think of me, and
take interest in me! I bowed down, and offered a prayer of thanks with tears of gratitude.

Blessings upon blessings be upon that somebody
who has not yet made his name known to me!

Nov. 26.—Visited David Brainard's tomb.

Nov. 28.—Read the life of David Brainard.
As I read his diaries, I felt as if I was reading
my own. When I came to the passage where
he says "that which makes all my difficulties
grievous to be borne, is that God hides his
face from me," I could not help crying. It
was, however, very consoling to think that I
am not the only one whom God disciplines
with goads internal and external. I yearned
after that sweet communion in heaven with
such blessed and tried spirits as his.

Dec. 4.—In morning at the President's class, I spoke how I came to believe Christianity as the Truth. I honestly and openly told the class how I came to find the conciliation of "moral schism" only in Christ, and closed my remarks with Luther's words, "I cannot do otherwise; God help me." Indeed, God helped me, and I felt throughout the day that I had done something honest and conscientious. Be instructed, O my Soul, that thou art to be a "witness" of what God hath done unto thee. Thou art not to proclaim to the world what thy little intellect has framed to thyself. Trust in the Lord, and be saved through *His* righteousness.

Our worthy President, like all true Christians, looked upon "heathen converts" with profound respect. (I speak this from my own experience). He told me, how early in 1859, when one of my countryman, a Christian, passed a night under his roof, he was so overtaken with the solemnity of the fact that "the Gentiles heard the Gospel," that he could not sleep all through the night. I was even afraid that he attached undue worth to us converted heathens, so much so that I had to frankly tell him once that any helps tendered me on account of my being a Christian must be declined by all means. But I was always willing to be of any service to him in his classes and prayer-meetings, as I knew he was not going to use me as a specimen of the tamed rhinoceros. That morning I was to confess myself, how without any hereditary influence, I came to embrace

Christianity as my faith. I did so right frankly, and I felt the better for having done so.

Dec. 5.—Much impressed by the thought that God's providence must be in my nation. If all good gifts are from Him, then some of the laudable characters of my countrymen must be also from on high. We must try to serve our God and the world with gifts and boons peculiar to ourselves. God does not want our national characters attained by the discipline of twenty centuries to be wholly supplanted by American and European ideas. The beauty of Christianity is that it can sanctify all the peculiar traits which God gave to each nation. A blessed and encouraging thought that *Japan too is God's nation.*

Dec. 23.—Took much thought about the means of paying my term bill.

Some of my readers may be curious to know how I got my living all these days. In several ways. My earnings in Pennsylvania, together with little story-telling with my awkward pen, kept me comfortable pretty nearly through the first year of my college existence. The good Dr. F., my teacher in Biblical Interpretation, once dropped one hundred dollars into my pocket, as from a friend of his, and told me "to come again" in time of need. Then I am ashamed to say, I showed myself a tamed rhinoceros about half-a-dozen times, and had some things given me in that way, but not much. Here let it be said in honor

of Christian America, that a heathen convert who
proposes to become a minister of the Gospel
among his countrymen, usually has no difficulty
about his bodily necessities, yea comforts, in that
land. But here hypocrisy creeps in, and some
Turks, Greeks, Armenians, Hindoos, Brazilians,
Chinese, Japanese, who really love their bellies
more than their God, feign themselves tamed rhinoceroses, and craftily indulge in the kindheart-
edness of the American Christians in that way.
And once in a while the home-churches are cautioned by their missionaries on the field of their
"promiscuous charity." They are told that those
converts whom they housed and educated while
they stayed with them, cast their Gospel into the
sea on their way home, entered government service or some others of Devil's service, and even
went so far as to malign Christendom before their
heathen countrymen.

But that is not the worst suspicion which a conscientious convert likes to avoid. He goes back
to his homeland, to preach the Gospel he learnt in
Christendom by charity. What say his countrymen of him and his Gospel? Why, they say
"there is money in that Gospel," and hoot him and
his Gospel off. Poor Convert! he is to sacrifice
the very Christian charity to which ne is entitled
by his other sacrifices, that he might win his kins-
men to Christ.

Under such circumstances, independence is pru-
dence, to say the least, and I made up my mind to
stick to it as much as possible. First of all, I cut
down my expense to a minimum, and tried to get
from the fresh air and God's Spirit whatever nutriment and comforts that were lacking in my
food and garnitures. For the first eighteen
months of my college days things went pretty

nearly as I calculated. But now, this my second
Christmas in New England, I had not seen a
greenback or a "We Trust in God" for a long
while. I fervently prayed for veritable manna
from heaven, but it did not come. I remembered
good Dr. F.'s words. I prayed again, made up my
mind, and waded through snow and slashes to his
home. O how the way appeared long to me that
night, though it was not more than a few hundred rods! Finally I came to the front of his
house, and gazed at the light in his study. Shall
I enter and ask for help? For ten long minutes
I stood amid snow, reflecting. What if my countrymen say that I lived by my religion? My
heart failed. I could proceed no further.
"Wait," I said finally to myself, and once more I
turned my lonely steps toward my room, now the
only lighted room upon the whole college hill. I
weighed two advantages, and found hunger pref-
erable to misunderstanding, both by my countrymen and other countrymen,—for the Gospel's
sake.

Jan. 5, 1887.—In evening, called upon Dr.
F. to ask for some monitary help. It was indeed a fiery trial. I could scarcely control
myself. But he was very kind to me, and
promised me to get some.

I had put off the trial, and tried to remove it
from me by my efforts during the Christmas recess. Indeed, necessity drove me to show myself
a tamed rhinoceros once or twice in some country
churches; but still there remained a considerable
deficit. The dilemma was now for me either to
tax American Christianity, or to remain in debt
to the mistress of my boarding house,—she a

good-hearted woman, recently widowed. While in this terrible dilemma, Providence sent me a help, not indeed in the form of the eatable manna as I expected, but in a thought which has ever since been of priceless value to me. In an old magazine that I took up during those drowzy hours, my eyes caught the following stanza, by one of America's sweetest singers, Adelaide A. Proctor:

"I hold him great who, for love's sake,
   Can give with generous, earnest will;
Yet he who takes for love's sweet sake
   I think I hold more generous still."

In the power of this song, I once more braved my way to the Doctor, laid my case before him, though tremblingly, and passed through the firey trial in that way. A few days after he fulfilled his promise, when I met him right in front of the town post office. It was near the dusk when one could hardly know another. The good man approached me, said a few kind words, thrust something into my pocket, and soon plodded away, leaving the world to darkness and to me.—Having had my bodily need supplied, I dived once more for the pearls of the Spiritual Truth.

Feb. 5.—Clear, cold.—There are cold days in spiritual world too. I try to warm my heart, to increase my love toward others, to make my prayers more earnest; but such efforts are like coal-fires in a cold weather, and are only partially and temporarily effectual. But once the warm and genial wind of the

Spirit blow, and how easy to warm my love, how earnest become my prayers, and how easy to be cheerful and satisfied! With all the efforts on our part, we are yet miserable sinners. There must come a Help supernatural to make us pure and holy.

Those piercing New England winters were severely felt by me, not so much on account of their biting effects upon my body, for I soon got accustomed to them, but because of their consumptive power of my precious coal. The very bricks of the dormitory building had to absorb heat from the poor student's stove before he got himself warmed thereby. But are there not some spiritual lessons too in this climatic phenomenon? The cheerless room is my heart when left by the Spirit of God, which howmuchsoever we heat is still cold. That genial wind from the direction of the Bermudas is His Spirit, which when it blows put all things to thawing, and relieves the poor student from the fear of coal bills. Blow, O Heavenly Zephyr, and let freezings cease in my heart and elsewhere.

April 15.—Morning Prayer: I come unto Thee, not because I am clean and pure and loving. I came unto Thee that I may be filled by Thee, so that I can pray to Thee more earnestly, love more, and be instructed more in Thy words and truth. Thou requirest me to feed on Thee, to possess Thee, the Fountain of all goodness, mercy, and love. Obedience, faithfulness, purity come only from Thee, and

I cannot produce them by the most strenuous efforts of mine. Thou orderest obedience to Thy laws, not because we are capable of so-doing by ourselves, but that by becoming conscious of our incapabilities, we may come unto Thee, and possess Thee. Thou hast given us Law that it may take us to Thee. So O Lord, acknowledging my total incapacity and depravity, I come unto Thee to be filled with Thy life. I am unclean; I pray *Thee* to cleanse me. I have no faith; give *Thou* me faith. Thou art Goodness Itself, and without Thee I am all darkness. Behold my foulness, and cleanse Thou me from my guiltiness. Amen.

April 23.—The Christian's prayer is not asking for his desires to be fulfilled by God's special interpositions. It is truly a communion with the Eternal Spirit, so that he is made to pray for what He hath already in His Mind. All prayers offered in such an attitude will and must be heard. The Christian's prayer is, therefore, a prophecy.

This I say is a considerable improvement upon my old heathen idea of prayer, which I am sorry to say, is still held by many under the Christian dispensation. I imagined, and many do still imagine, that God can be so prevailed upon with our prayers that the very laws of Nature can be reversed thereby. Not so, my Soul. Conform thy will to His which always meaneth good, and

thou shalt cease to wrestle in impossible prayers
to stop the sun in its course, and get more light
and pleasure therefrom.

With reflections like these, my New England
college days came to close. I entered it in heavi-
ness of heart, and left it with triumphant glory-
ings in my Lord and Savior. Since then I studied
more and learnt more, but only to corroborate
what I learnt upon the classic hill of my college.
I believe I was really converted, that is turned
back, there, some ten years after I was baptized
in my homeland. The Lord revealed Himself to
me there, especially through that one man,—the
eagle-eyed, lion-faced, lamb-hearted president of
my college. The Spirit within me, examples before me, and Nature and things around me, sub-
jugated me at last. Of course the complete sub-
jugation is the work of life-time; but I was right-
ed so far as to depend no more upon vain efforts
of mine in subjugating myself, but to have recourse to the Power of the Universe for that end.
A little god of the world,—he is subjugatable only
by the Almighty Power Itself.

As for my intellectual gains in my college, they
amounted to but very little; or at least they appeared so in comparison with what I gained in
my spirit. A student whose mind is so much
taken up with the salvation of his own soul, and
not a little about the sustenance of his body, cannot be expected to make much progress in his
study. But the college dealt with me very leni-
ently, indeed munificently. Though I entered it
as a special student, and hence was not entitled
to any organic relation with it, they adopted me,
and gave me a place among her genuine sons, and
the boys gave me three yells for the honor thus
conferred upon me. Thus I was made to live

nobly and honorably, not only for my religion and country, but for my alma mater as well. The "college-spirit," outside of baseball grounds, is a noble and Christian sentiment, which if loyally stuck to, should alone be sufficient to keep her sons from demagogism, cloth-worship, man-face-fearing, and meannesses and unmanlinesses of very many kinds in this world. I understand the spirit of my college to be noble independence, brave defiance of hollow shows of all kinds, patient and reverential search after Truth, orthodoxy in anti-head-religion sense of the term, and not published Paganism, not the religion of "the greatest probability," not "success" in its vulgar nineteenth century sense. I am exceedingly thankful that I was given another such mother to serve and satisfy. May I live worthy of her name and glory!

I stayed during two long months of the summer vacation alone in the dormitory, now deserted by its turbulent occupants, to prepare myself for entrance to a theological seminary in the coming Fall. The time thus spent was the best I have had in my life. Serene loneliness, beautiful natural surroundings, constant presence of God's Spirit within me, reflections upon Past and Future,—indeed the whole hill was beautified into a Zion, a Home of my God. Here is the record of one of those happy days:

Aug. 27.—Clear, delightful day.—Calm. Often feel very lonely, but I rest upon my God. I asked my soul what shall she do if God take away my life right now. She answered: "I shall rejoice even though He slay me. God's will will surely be carried out even though I be destroyed. The consecrated soul rejoices only in the glorification of God, and not in its own success."

Sept. 12.—The last day in A.—A very impressive day. I thought of many struggles and temptations I met here during the last two years. I also thought of many triumphant victories I have gained over my sin and weakness by God's help, and of many glorious revelations from Him. Indeed, my whole life has been directed toward new paths, in which I can now proceed with hope and courage. May God's choicest blessings accompany this hallowed hill!—Went to see President to say good-bye. As usual, tears came to my eyes when I stood before that venerable man, and I had but very little to say, because I had so much to say. After giving me some advice, he handed me one hundred dollars to help me in my further career, and then dismissed me with rich blessing. Tears burst into my eyes, and I spoke to him some sobbing words. Lord knoweth how much I think of that man. He did me everything, and now after receiving my education, diploma, and many other things, I go away with $—— as a "balance," as he said! O my Soul, be sure to open thy purse and heart freely to the poor and afflicted when Lord will intrust thee with money and grace.—When I returned to my room, I found three swallows straying into it, because the night was dark and boisterous outside. They flapped their wings furiously against the walls. I gently caught the timid creatures, and though I was afraid of sending them into darkness, I dared not to keep them in my room, because they were afraid of my presence. So after commending them to the merciful care of the Father of the Universe, I sent them away.

The next day, I left my college-town, and came to my seminary.

CHAPTER IX.

IN CHRISTENDOM.—A DIP INTO THEOLOGY.

It was after long-continued fearful struggles that I finally submitted myself to become a theologue. I told you before that I was born in a soldier family, and soldiers with all practical men despise pedantries and sentimentalities of all kinds. And what class of men are usually more unpractical than priests? The wares they deal out to this busy society are what they call sentiments,—those uncertain nothings manufacturable by the worst sluggard in the world,—for which they get in return food, clothing, and other things of real and substantial worth. So we say priests live by charity, and we believed sword to be more honorable means of existence than charity.

To be a priest is bad enough; but to be a Christian priest I considered to be the end of my doom. In a heathen country like mine, Christian ministers are supported either directly or indirectly by foreigners, and are to place themselves under the jurisdiction of foreign bishops of one kind or the other. As no true German suffers himself to be ruled by an Italian or a French priest, so no true countryman of mine suffers himself to be shackled by a foreign influence of any kind. To call in an aid of economic principles, like *Laissez faire* and *Quid pro quo*, to deliver oneself from this conscientious regard for national honor, we consider to be a baseness, and even a danger to our national independence. Thought is cosmopolitan, and we are glad, yea thankful, to be taught by all men of all nations. But not so bread. The fact is, the bondage of mind is not the most dangerous kind of bondage; but that of stomach is. France had great Frederick's mind in bondage; but it was he who delivered Germany from French domination. Prussia had Voltaire's stomach in bondage; and behold his misery and degradation. Cosmopolitanism in the sphere of things is always a vicious principle.

Thus in my case Christian priesthood meant a bondage of double nature; and honor for myself and honor for my country had kept me from conceiving any idea whatever of entering into Christian ministerial service. Indeed, the first and greatest fear I had when I was first induced to accept Christianity was that they might make a priest out of me. And afterward when my enthusiasm in religious works called forth the attention of my Christian friends, and made them think that my probable mission in this life might be preaching, I rejected their suggestions with oaths and fistings. Professional clergymen I hated from the bottom of my heart, and I was perfectly wild when any of my friends persuaded me to become one.

But this life-long prejudice against priesthood was greatly mitigated by my contact with clergymen of high and noble order. The worthy President of my New England college was a clergyman and theologian. The Methodist minister from whom I received baptism was a clergyman of most admiring character; and I always excepted him when I indulged in my usual denunciations of priest-class. Dr. F., my teacher in the Biblical Interpretation, Dr. B., our college-pastor, and others,—they were all clergymen, and were *not* humbugs and traders in wind. I came to see that clergymen are sometimes the most useful members of society, that it does pay to have a good minister, that they are here upon this earth doing something, and many a time, great things.

Was not Luther too a clergyman, though not a common clergyman? Was not John Knox, that valiant idol-breaker, a clergyman and theologian? Were not some of the world's greatest warriors too thoughtful students of Theology? John Hampden, my ideal gentleman and Christian, though an Englishman he,—was not his heroic deed the result of his profound theologic convictions? Gaspar de Coligny,—was his Theology of no account to him in forming his gigantic schemes for the renovation of his beloved France? If Theology was a plaything and a sorcerer's cup of the world's greatest liars and hypocrites, has it not also been the employment of the world's mightiest intellects, and the discipliner of the world's noblest souls? If, as its etymology indicates, Theology is the science of God, what true sons of Adam can excuse themselves from the reverential study of the same? What science of God's Universe is not Theology? And what actions of man can be right and true if not guided by the science of God? O my Soul, be thou a theologue then. Deliver it from the hand of hypocrites and spiritual quacks, as David did God's Ark from the hand of the Philistines. The science itself is the noblest of all; man only is vile who leaves it in the hand of "heathens."

The daily increasing sense of reality of spiritual experiences helped me to dispel all the notions of hollowness and non-utility which I had once attached to Theology. Indeed I saw the reason of

my hatred of Theology. If spirit *is* real, as rice
and potatoes are real, why despise Theology and
praise Agriculture? If it is noble to grow corn,
and feed myself and my hungering fellowmen
with the fruits of God's Earth, why ignoble to
learn of His Laws to appropriate His Spirit to our
hungering souls, and be made nobler and manlier
thereby? Agriculture that raises only husks and
straw, and gives them out to the public as real
wheat and rice, we despise and hoot at. That
indeed is no Agriculture, but it is Rock-Culture
and Sand-Culture, which really feed nobody. So
Theology I have been reviling at is No-Theology.
It was Demonology, that gives out wind in place
of spirit, rhetoric in place of sermon, and sound
in place of music. Theology is substantial, eatable and drinkable,—so substantial, so nutritious
that whosoever drinketh of the water it giveth
shall not thirst, and whosoever eateth of the flesh
it giveth shall not hunger. Ashamed of Theology? Yes, be thou forever ashamed of No-Theology, of Demonology, be it taught in Theological
Seminaries or other institutions; but of Theology
proper, wherever taught, be thou proud. The
world that holds in honor the names of George
Peabody and Stephen Girard, who freely gave out
their perishable possessions for the relief of the
poor and hungry, will continue to revere the
names of Neander and Julius Muller and others
of their kind, who systematized our religious
thought, and made good-doing and God-serving
almost a scientific possibility. "Heart is the centre of Theology," said the father of the Church
History, and he that has no heart, but stomach
only, should stand outside of it.

Thus persuaded, I made up my mind to study
Theology, but upon one important condition; and

that was that *I should never be licensed,* I said in my heart, "Lord, I shall study Theology if Thou compellest me not to be a reverend. Should I succeed to take in all the theologies of Christendom, I shall not add to my name that ponderous title designated by double D's. From that Thou must release me for this final sacrifice of mine." He said Yea, and upon that agreement I entered a Theological Seminary.

Sept. 18. Sunday.—If Theology is a science in which there is nothing real and practical, it is not worth studying. True Theology, however, is something real, yea, more real than any other science. Medicine alleviates physical sufferings of man; Jurisprudence treats of the civil relations of man to man; but Theology looks into the very cause of physical diseases and civil disorders. The true Theologian is naturally an idealist, but he is not a dreamer. The realization of his idea lies many centuries in future. His work is like contributing a brick or two into a massive building which takes an infinite number of years to be completed. He puts his hand upon it, only believing that honest and faithful works will never be lost.

Sept. 19.—Theology is too big a theme to be comprehended by small men. When small minds find themselves too small for such a gigantic theme, they construct their own theologies fitting their own smallness, and throw anathemas at those who comprehend it better than they. O my Soul, do not contract Theology to fit thy smallness, but expand thyself to fit its largeness.

Oct. 12.—Rather disgusted with works in the recitation rooms. We discussed upon hell and purgatory in New Testament exegesis, and on equally unsubstantial subjects in Apolegetics. Spiritless Theology is the driest and most worthless of all studies. To see students laughing and jesting while discussing serious subjects is almost shocking. No wonder they cannot get at the bottom of the Truth. It requires the utmost zeal and earnestness to draw life from the Rock of Ages.

Nov. 3.—I am seeking for a higher type of morality than "must." I am hungering after the morality that cometh from God's grace. But such a morality is denied not only by the majority of mankind, but very little seems to be believed in by the students and professors of theological seminaries. I do not hear anything new and different within these sacred walls from those which I hear outside. Confucius and Buddha can teach me the largest part of what these theologues are presuming to teach to the heathen.

Nov. 7.—What is this world? It is a scene of universal enmity and dissension. Infidelity versus Christianity, Roman Catholicism versus Protestantism, Unitarianism versus Orthodoxy,—mankind pitches its tent, one part against another part, one section of one part against another section of the same part,— each trying to benefit itself by the mistakes and failures of others. Not only are individuals not to be trusted, but mankind as a whole are generations of vipers, manhaters, descendants of Cain. O my soul, away from isms, be they Methodism or Congregationalism, or any other high-sounding isms. Seek the Truth, quit thyself like a man, cease from men, and look above thee.

Nov. 18.—Am reading Life of David Hume. My religious enthusiasm is cooled down by coming in contact with the cool mind of this acute philospher. But I am willing to test my religious experiences in rigorous scientific ways. I want to be intellectually certain that I am not dwelling in "the Fata Morgana of philosophic dreamland." In this age of progress of physical science, it won't do to get rid of doubters with anathemas. Religion must be objectivized, made "tangible" and scientifically comprehensible. Yet alas! I see around me the trodding of the same old paths, each trying to excel the other how to ape the good old ministers who were "very much liked by their parishioners."

Dec. 5.—In every man's life there is a sort of paradigm divinely appointed beforehand. His success consists in conforming himself to this paradigm, neither coming short of it, nor exceeding it. In it alone is perfect peace. His body and mind can be used to the best possible advantage when he walks *in* it. Lack of ambition often keeps him short of it, and he goes away from this world without accomplishing his work to the utmost of his capacity. On the other hand, too much ambition causes him to overleap it; hence shattered system and premature death. Man's selective power (free-will) lies in conforming himself to this paradigm. Once he puts himself in the current, then his efforts are no more spent in propelling him forward, but only in keeping him *in* the current. Take up, enjoy any blessings that lie in this current, but never go *out* of it to hunt after them. Dare through any obstacle which obstructs this current, for it cannot be an immovable mountain, since God appointed the way. For all this, trust not thyself. God hath appointed thy current; He also hath appointed a Captain for thee. "Hear ye *Him!*"

Dec. 29.—I feel ashamed that I am still ashamed sometimes before others of my studying Theology. The fact is, the worldly-minded cannot see the spiritual side of any study, and of course the idea of preaching for the sake of bread and butter must appear to them extremely mean. The real self-sacrifice of becoming a true preacher of the Gospel lies in the fact that the self-sacrifice does not look like a self-sacrifice to the mass of mankind. Yea more, it does look like the greatest possible meanness to them. Not so with practical charity and kind deeds of other sorts. To hide it (study of Theology) as much as possible from those who consider it a sacrifice, and to confess it before those who consider it a meanness,—ah yes, the Christian must go on a pretty thorny path in this world. Indeed, narrow is the way that is alloted to the children of the Cross. Father, forgive my open denials of Thee before men, and give me more courage and confidence in my calling.

But I was not to continue my study of Theology any further. Severe mental strains of the past three years unsettled my nerves, and chronic insomnia of a most fearful kind took hold of me.

Rest, bromides, prayers proved ineffectual, and the only way now open for me was one leading toward my homeland. I was to quit Theology, and to go home with whatever gains I had made during my exile in foreign lands.

Further recollections showed me, however, the wisdom and reasonableness of such an order of Providence. American seminaries, established expressly to train young men for American churches, are not the fittest places to train one destined for fields otherwise circumstanced than that country. Besides the exegetical studies of the Old and New Testaments, much that is taught in these seminaries may be dispensed with without detracting much from the usefulness of practical workers in missionary lands. Not that Pastoral and Historical and Dogmatic and Systematic Theologies are of no moment to us, for I sincerely believe there is no branch of the human knowledge which the Christian need not know; but the question is that of *comparative* importance. Not sceptic Hume, nor analytic Baur are we to grapple with, but with the subtilities of Hindoo philosophies, the non-religiosities of Chinese moralists, together with the confused thoughts and actions of new-born nations, materialistic in their new aspirations, but spiritualistic in their fundamental conceptions. "Church" in the common acceptation of the term as used by the Occidental Christians is wholly unknown among my countrymen, and it is yet a grave question whether this institution, valuable though it doubtless is in other countries, can be planted with any hope of stability among the people to whom I belong. The method of moral and religious teachings to which we have been accustomed during twenty centuries of our national existence is not that of sermonizing upon texts and delivery from pulpits. With us we make no distinctions between moral and intellectual trainings. The school is our church, and we are expected to bring up our whole beings in it. Idea of speciality in religion sounds extremely odd, and even repulsive, to our ears. Priests we have, but they are essentially temple-keepers, and not teachers in Truth and Eternal Verities. All our moral reformers were teachers, "pedagogues," who taught in things of spirit while they taught in letters and science. "Knowledge is of worth as it enlightens ways of righteousness. Man applies himself to its acquisition *not* to become a professional moralist thereby." So said Takayama Hikokuro, that eccentric heathen Japanese, and it was he, together with many such as he, that wrought the grandest and noblest reform, moral, political, and otherwise, that that island empire has ever witnessed.

And what about means and arts of soul-converting, church-member-making, and other similar business? A soul converted to Christianity by means and arts can be reconverted to heathenism also by means and arts. We in this materialistic century make too much out of environments. Darwinism seems to have converted Christianity at last. Good choirs, pleasant church sociables, young ladies' bazars, free lunches, Sunday-school picnics,—all such are now considered as *important means* to keep up spirit, and much of "Pastoral Theology" seems to be occupied with such business. And if polished Rhetoric is more coveted by young theologues than Fire,—and even that Fire for Rhetoric's sake,—and if preachers' sermons are talked about more from the elocutionary and dramatic standpoints of view than from their fire-setting and idol-breaking aspects, well might Chrysostom curse his tongue that delivered heavenly oracles with golden resonance, and Augustine despise Rhetoric as an art of deception. If, as critics tell us, St. Paul was not the handsomest of men, and his Greek not the purest of its kind; if Bossuet's eloquence and Masillon's finished style could not revert the onslaught of the French Revolution; if Bunyan a tinker and Moody a store clerk could make as good preachers of Gospel Truth as their ages could wish,—then need I not be sorry that I was not able to finish my training in a theological seminary.

I told you that I came to my seminary upon an agreement that I should never be licensed. Some of my good friends were sorry of my quitting theological study without having gone with it so far as to get a license. With me, however, license was the thing I was seriously afraid of. And the fear that I had entertained about the bestowal of this new privilege upon me grew more as I observed its benefits talked about within the walls of my seminary. "One thousand dollars with parsonage," "twenty dollars' sermon upon Chicago anarchy," and similar combinations of such words and phrases sounded very discordantly to my ears. That sermons have market-values, as porks and tomatoes and pumpkins have, is not an Oriental idea at least. We Orientals are very suspicious set of people. So remarked John Stuart Mill, and compared us to Catholic Spaniards. And none we suspect more than one who has religion for sale. With us, religion is *not* usually convertible into cash. Indeed, more religion, *less* cash. Superstitious as we are, we cannot yet reconcile Religion with Political Economy. And if license seals market-values upon our religion, happy am I if I am not so sealed, for I thus escape from the temptation.

Indeed, this matter of paid ministry is yet a much mooted question with us. Our heathen teachers used to have no stipulated pays for their services. Twice every year, their pupils brought to them whatever did lie in the power of each to bring. From ten pieces of gold to a bundle of parsnips or carrots, were gradations of such "tokens of gratitude," as they were called. They had no deacons to poke them to death for church-dues and pew-rents, and other such things. A teacher was expected to remain as no-teacher till he had made enough progress in his spiritual disciplines as to be able to rely entirely upon heaven and his fellowmen for the support of his body. This they considered a most practical method of "natural selection," no danger thus of being imposed upon with pseudo-teachers and time-servers.

I grant that man does not live by spirit alone, but by every thing that springs out of the ground as well. This is an argument for paid ministry, and we consider it an entirely fair argument. Our present-day Physiology deduces forces mental and forces spiritual from pieces of bread and mutton; and why not upon the principle of "Transmutability of Energy" exchange spirit *for mutton?* Starvation of our bodies is no less a sin than that of our souls. Divine laws of health require that head-working and heart-taxing ministers of Gospel be properly and nicely fed and clothed.

The poor exacting Orientals cannot, however, see into this simple scientific argument. They do believe that man does not live by bread alone; that spirit somehow is a bodily food as well, and that mutton-chops and chicken-pies *can* be dis-

pensed with by those who live with the plenitude
of heavenly spirit in them. Hence "unkind" crit-
icisms upon the ways of missionaries' living. Of
course these missionaries do not live in "palatial
styles," as sometimes reported by the enemies of
Missions. They only live as they live in their
own lands. But to the people among whom they
are sent, they do appear to live palatially. You
know wealth and comforts are only comparative
terms, and a lounge is a luxury to one who rolls
upon a straw-mat. Herein comes, therefore, one
barrier through which missionaries' zeal had to
work pretty hard, in order to reach the perishing
heathens with the glad tidings of salvation.

And once in a while come some "blessed" missionaries, who, looking into this idiosyncracy of
heathens, comport themselves accordingly. They
strip off their white neckties, have their heads pig-
tailed, deny themselves of pies and other home-
delicacies, learn to bend their legs upon straw-
mats, and in all ways and diverse manners, go
into their earnest business of winning souls to
Jesus. To such we heathens bear with gladness.
They help us wonderfully in coming to Light and
Truth, and we bless them and Him that sent them
for the good they do unto us. Such a missionary
was one Mr. Crossett, a Presbyterian missionary
to China. He became a Chinaman himself, and
that not a Mandarin kind of Chinamen. Finally
his "eccentricity" deprived him of home-support;
but he had heathens themselves to help his works
on. He started poor-houses in Pekin, supported
by heathen Pekinese merchants. He travelled
in steerage with average Chinamen. While thus
on his mission over the Yellow Sea, the call to his
high home came to him. The remonstrance of the
ship's captain to him to come to his cabin and

there lie in comfort was gently declined, as he would like to die among the people to whom he was sent. They forced him to the cabin, and there he expired, commending all around him to his God and Savior. The news of his death reached his homeland. Religious papers passed it over without much comment upon it. Yea more. Cases were cited tacitly proving that his sacrifice was a foolish sacrifice, that good can be done in the first-class cabin, with white neck-ties on. Yet Pekinese and Tentsinese and other pig-tailed gentlemen do not forget his service. They gave him the name of "Christian Buddha,"—so hallowed was his presence among them. Of his religion perhaps very few of them benefited themselves; but of him all had to learn something about divine sorrow and love.

A fortunate missionary he! Perhaps not everybody can imitate him. Perhaps his stomach was that of an ostrich, that could digest Chinamen's food without dyspeptic effects. I say he was fortunate, because such as he need not complain of "the difficulty of the station." We will not try to ape him, because aping is hypocrisy, and no good comes out of it. Pigtailing and steeraging are *not* the essence of the matter, of course; but his spirit *is,* which we will not despise as an "eccentricity." We will pray to be made like him, if any of us are ever ambitious to be successful missionaries among heathens.

But this adaptability to all surroundings is not to be acquired by seminary trainings. Such trainings do indeed adapt us to wrong surroundings, from which it is extremely difficult to un-adapt ourselves. Many a case do I know of my own countrymen, who have adapted themselves to Occidental ways of life and thought during such

trainings, and coming home as strangers, has each to re-adapt himself to his former surroundings with the utmost difficulty. Boiled rice and smashed beans do not afford him all the nutriment his newly-adapted system requires, and sittings upon hard straw-mats cause synovitis and other troubles of his lower limbs. His throat suffers, because native churches have no steam-heaters to take off chill from the air, and his head rings, because the ventilation is poor. The least he needs is greatest in the eyes of his people. He loses flesh, and with flesh, spirit. Preaching becomes unbearable. To some other occupations he betakes himself, and others hardier than he take his place. Struggle for existence is too much for him.—Then his method of thought: how incompatible it too has become with that of his countrymen! He denounces Hume-ism and Theodore-Parker-ism; but Hume and Parker have had no existence in the minds of the people to whom he is preaching. The downfall of the Roman Empire and the persecutions of Bloody Mary sound as "wind to the horse's ear," as we term all incomprehensibilities. He proves Biblical truths by the Bible; but the Bible is no more to these people than some sooty parchments of idle antiquarians. His sermons fly over their heads and vanish into the air. He is disappointed with his hearers, and his hearers with him. Dissatisfaction, grumbling, resignation, separation. Should we make princes to send to beggars? * * *

But these are only the negative aspects of seminary life, which I called forth to my reflections to console myself in the misfortune of the hour. The positive benefits of theological training need not be counted here in detail. If a seminary cannot *make* a prophet,—for the prophet, like the poet, *is born,*—it is the very best place for him to grow and develop. If it is not an abode of angels, —for such is nowhere to be found in this nether world,—it is a purer and holier association than any under heaven. The very fact that its defects stand out in stronger reliefs than those of any other institutions, proves the light shining therein to be brighter and more searching. Poor theologues, they stand in the greatest disadvantage in their attitude toward this criticism-loving generation. The world expects from them what it can expect only from angels; it throws stones at them, while it is guilty of the very same sins it condemns in them. Mammonism it openly and Political-Economically follows, it reviles in the ministers of Gospel. Let Christian ministers, missionaries, repent in ashes and sackclothes toward their Almighty God and Savior; but toward men, they as a class need not feel ashamed. We of the King's household make so much of failings which in the outsider's estimate are not worth a moment's reflection. Let not the commotion in Zion be construed by them as similar in nature to howlings and gnashings of teeth in their own Mammondom.

I left my seminary to retrace my steps toward my homeland.

CHAPTER X.

THE NET IMPRESSIONS OF CHRISTENDOM.— RETURN HOME.

Now that my disciplines in Christendom came to end, my readers would like to know what I think of it after all. Did I retain to the last the impressions I received on my first landing upon it? Is Christendom after all better than Heathendom? Is Christianity worth introducing to my country; or is there *raison d'etre* of Christian mission?

First let me frankly confess that I was not entirely taken up by Christendom. Three-and-a-half years' stay in it, with the best of hospitality it gave me, and the closest of friendships I formed in it, did not entirely naturalize me to it. I remained a stranger throughout, and I never had exerted myself to be otherwise. Not as Terra-del-Fuegians in a civilized country yearn after their former roamings over the foamy cliffs under the Southern Cross, or as latinized Indians seek for re-companionship with buffaloes in their native prairies, but with aims higher and nobler I yearned after my homeland with "Home-Sweet-Home" yearnings till the very last of my stay in Christendom. Never have I entertained any wish whatever of becoming an American or an Englishman; but I rather reckoned my heathen relationship a special privilege of my own, and thanked God once and again for having brought me out into this world as a "heathen," and not as a Christian.

For there are several advantages to be born a heathen. Heathenism I consider as an undeveloped stage of humanity, developable into a higher and perfecter stage than that attained by any form of Christianity. There are perennial hopes in heathen nations still untouched by Christianity; hopes as of the youth venturing for life grander than that of all his predecessors. And though my nation is more than two thousand years old in History, it is yet a child in Christ, and all the hopes and possibilities of future lie shrouded in its rapidly developing days. Thrice thankful am I that I can witness many such days. Then I could feel the power of the New Truth more. What to the "born Christians" sounded as time-worn commonplaces, were to me new revelations, and called forth from me all the praises sung perhaps by our first parents, when,

> " 'neath a curtain of translucent dew,
> Bathed in the rays of the great setting flame,
> Hesperus, with the host of heaven, came,
> And lo! creation widened in man's view."

In myself I could witness the changes and progress of the eighteen Christian centuries, and when I came out of all my strifes, I found myself a sympathetic man, acquainted as I was with all the stages of spiritual development from idol-worship up to soul's emancipation in the Crucified Son of God. Such visions and experiences are not vouchsafed to all of God's children, and we who are called in the eleventh hour have at least this privilege to make up for all the loss of having remained in darkness so long.

In forming any right estimate of Christendom, it is essential for us first of all to make a rigid distinction between Christianity pure and simple, and Christianity garnished and dogmatized by its professors. I believe no sane man of this generation dare speak ill of Christianity itself. After reading all the skeptic literature that had come to my hand, I came to the conclusion that Jesus of Nazareth remains untouched after all the furious attacks made upon those who are called by His name. If Christianity is what I now believe it to be, it is as firm and fixed as the Himalaya itself. He that attacks it does so to his own disadvantage. Who but fools dare rush at rocks? Some indeed rush at what they imagine to be Christianity, which in fact is no Christianity, but superstructures over the same, built by some faithless believers, who, thinking that the Rock by itself cannot stand all the wear and tear of Time, shed it over with shrines, cathedrals, churches, doctrines, Thirty Nine Articles, and other structures of combustible nature; and some fools of this world, knowing that such are combustible, set fire to them, and rejoice over their conflagration, and think that the Rock itself has also vanished in the flame. Behold the Rock is there, "towering o'er the wrecks of Time."

But what is Christianity? Certainly it is not the Bible itself, though much of it, and perhaps the essence of it, is contained *in* it. Neither can it be any set of dogmas framed by men to meet the exigencies of a time. Really we know more of what it is not than what it is.

We say Christianity is Truth. But that is defining an undefinable by another undefinable. "What is Truth?" is asked by the Roman Pilate and other unveracious men. Truth, like Life, is hardest, yea impossible, to be defined; and this mechanical century has begun to doubt both because of their undefinability. Bichat, Treviranus, Beclard, Huxley, Spencer, Haeckel, each has his own definition of Life; but all unsatisfactory. "Organization in action," says one; "the sum total of the forces which resist death," says another. But we know it is more. *The true knowledge of Life ocmes only by living it.* Scalpel and Microscope show only the mechanism of it.—So Truth. We come to know it only by keeping it. Logic-chopping, hair-splitting, and wire-drawing only make it less true. Truth is there, unmistakable, majestic; and we have but to go there from ourselves, and not call it to us. The very attempt to define Truth shows our own stupidity, for what but the Infinite Universe can define or limit Truth? So we shall give up the definition of Truth, if for the mere purpose of hiding our own stupidity.

So I came to see that the undefinability of Christianity is not an evidence of its non-existence, much less of its humbugness. The very fact that it grows more to me the more I conform myself to its teachings, shows its close relationship with the Infinite Truth itself. I know it is *not* a thing wholly unrelated to other religions. It is *one* of "ten great religions," and we will not, like some, depreciate all others to make it appear as the only religion that is worth having. But to me it is more, very much more, than any religion that I am acquainted with. At least it is perfecter than the religion in which I was brought up, and now after sifting all that has been lectured upon "Comparative Religion," I can yet think of nothing perfecter than it.

"But no more panegyrics," you say. "Tell us in what respect it is perfecter than your heathenism."

Heathenism, like much of what passes for Christianity in Christendom, teaches morality, and inculcates upon us the keeping of the same. It shows us the way, and commands us to walk therein. No more and no less. As for Juggernaut, infant-sacrifice, and so forth, let us eliminate them from our account of heathenism, for they are not it, as mammon-worship, and infant-killing by other methods than that of throwing them to gavials, and other horrors and superstitions of Christendom are not Christianity. Therein let us be fair and forgiving in judging others. We will meet our enemy in his best and strongest.

I do not hesitate to say that Christianity does the same; i. e., shows us the way to walk in. Indeed, it does so more clearly and unmistakably than any other religion. In it there is no will-of-the-wisp-ness of the guiding light that I often meet with in other faiths. Indeed, one prominent feature of Christianity is this sharpness of distinction between Light and Darkness, Life and Death. But let any fair judge compare the Ten Commandments of Moses with those of Buddha, and he will see at once that the difference is not that of day from night. "The Rectitude of Life" as taught by Buddha, Confucius, and other "heathen" teachers, is something, which if carefully studied by Christians, will make them ashamed of their former self-satisfaction. Do but make the Chinese and the Japanese keep the commandments of their own Confucius, and you make fairer Christendoms out of these two nations than any you have in Europe or America. The best of Christian converts has never given up the essence of Buddhism-or-Confucianism. We welcome-Christianity, because it helps us to become more like our own ideals. Only zealots,

"revivalists," pleasers of some show-loving missionaries, indulge in the auto-da-fe of the objects
of their former worship. "I came to fulfill, and
not to destroy," said the Founder of Christianity.

Christianity is more and higher than Heathenism *in that it makes us keep the law.* It is Heathenism *plus* Life. By it alone the law-keeping
becomes a possibility. It is the Spirit of the Law.
It of all religions works from inside. It is what
Heathenism has been searching and groping after
with much weeping. It not only shows us the
Good, but it makes us good by taking us right at
once to the Eternal Goodness Himself. It pro-
vides us not only with the Way, but with the Life
as well; with the Rail as well as with the Engine.
I am yet to be taught by "Comparative Religion"
of some other religion that does likewise.*

With the "Philosophy of the Plan of Salvation"
let Philosophical Wisdom concern itself to its
heart's content. The *fact* of salvation is there,
and Philosophy or No-Philosophy cannot unmake
facts. The human experience has yet known of
no other name under heaven given among men,
whereby we must be saved. Of moral science we
have more than enough. That any Ph. D. can tell
us, if we but pay big fees to him. We know we
must not steal, without a doctor to teach us. But
oh not to steal, in the manifold and spiritual sense

---

* The Right Honorable William Ewart Gladstone's
definition of Christianity is this:

"Christianity in the established Christian sense, is
the presentation to us, not of abstract dogmas for acceptance, but of a living and a Divine Person, to whom
we are to be united by a vital incorporation. It is the
reunion to God of a nature severed from God by sin, and
the process is one, not of teaching lessons, but of impart-
ing a new life, with its ordained equipment of gifts and
powers."—From Criticism on "Robert Elsmere."

of stealing! "Look at me, and be ye saved." "As Moses lifted up the serpent in the wilderness, even so must the Son of Man be lifted up; that whosoever believeth in him should not perish, but have eternal life." In this looking at Him is our salvation, whatever be the philosophy of it. The nineteen Christian centuries teach me so, and my little soul too can testify (God be thanked) that it is so.

This then is Christianity. It is at least so to me. Deliverance from sin by the atoning grace of the Son of God. It may be more, but it cannot be less. This the essence of Christianity then; and popes and bishops and reverends and other adjuncts, useful and otherwise, are *not* the necessary parts of it. As such it is worth having above all other things. No true man can get along without it, and Peace cannot be his without it.

Webster defines Christendom as "that portion of the world in which Christianity prevails, or which is governed under Christian institutions, in distinction from heathen or Mohammedan lands." He does not say it is a land of perfected angels. It is where Christianity prevails, or is looked up to by the majority of the people as the guide of their lives. Two elements, Belief and Believers, determine the practical morality of any nation. Fierce Saxons, piratical Scandinavians, pleasure-loving French, trying to manage themselves in this world by the tenets of the Divine Man of Nazareth,—that is what we witness in Christendom. Lay no blame then upon Christianity for *their* untowardness; but rather praise it for its subduing power over tigers such as they. What if these people had no Christianity? What if no Pope Leos are with them to curb their depredations, and turn them over to Justice and

Forgiveness? Buddhism and Confucianism will be to them as Apollinaris' Water is to chronic dyspepsia,—inertness, insipidity, the return of animalism, eternal destruction. It is only by the Church Militant arrayed against the huge monstrosities of mammonism, rum-traffic, Louisiana lottery, and other enormities, that Christendom is kept from precipitating into immediate ruin and death. A son of a Presbyterian minister, by the name of Robert Ingersoll, said that it would be better for his country to turn all of its churches into theatres. He said so because he was sure that his country would never follow his advice. Say whatever we may of the "beastliness" of Christendom; does not its very disease testify to the vitality of the Life that keeps it alive?

Then observe this optic phenomenon of *the greatest darkness with the greatest light.* The shadow is the deeper, the brighter the light that casts it. One characteristic of Truth is that it makes the bad worse and the good better. It is useless to ask why this is so. "For whosoever hath, to him shall be given, and he shall have more abundance: but whosoever hath not, from him shall be taken away even that he hath;"—in morals as in economics. The same sun that melts wax hardens clay. If Christianity is light unto all men, it is not to be wondered at that it develops badness as well as goodness. We may reasonably expect therefore the worst badness in Christendom.

It is said that the state of New York with a population of 5,000,000 produces more murderers than Japan with 40,000,000 souls. General Grant's observation in the latter country was that the number and state of its poor were nothing compared with what he saw in his own United

States.   London is proverbial for the magnitude
of its pauperism, and Christendom generally for
its gambling and drinking habits.   Some of the
alcoholic liquors that can satisfy the appetite of
these people are strong enough to upset the heads
of our drunkards, if taken in any considerable
quantity.   Scenes in those back streets of some
of the largest cities of Christendom, which no
decent men dare even to look into, can be described with no milder words than the vilest in
any language.   Shameless gamblings, open-day
piracies, cool-blooded sacrifice of fellowmen for
one's own aggrandizement, are being conducted
there on gigantic, business-like scales.   You who
look with pity upon heathens, and glory in the
blessedness of your Christian civilization, read
with fair open eyes the following that came to
my ears from one of your own philanthropists:

In the suburb of the capital city of one of the
most Christian of Christian countries, lived in
silence an old couple, in apparent enjoyment of
the good things of this world.   The cause of their
wellbeing remained a secret to themselves alone.
One thing peculiar, however.   They had a stove
which to all outward appearances was altogether
too large for their cooking purposes; and the
chimney-pipe smoked late in the stillness of night,
when no man eats, but all go to sleep.   The quaint
little household called forth the attention of a
heroic woman of the city, who with her keen
womanly instinct combined a tact of the most
practical kind when in pursuit of the dark things
of the world.   She investigated the case carefully,
quietly.   Evidences upon evidences were secured,
and further skepticism became impossible.   One
dark night, she with proper authorities breaks
into the house.   The stove is the object of sus-

picion. They open it, and what do you think they
find in there? Embers of anthracites to cheer
the old age? No. The horror of horrors! Human-
looking things there! Supple babies being baked!
The price of baking, two dollars a piece! Engaged in this business for twenty years unmo-
lested! and made quite a fortune out of it, too!
For what purpose this horror? To cover and
annihilate the shame that called the unlucky
babies into being! The city too full of illegiti-
macies; hence the prosperity of the old couple's
trade! And my narrator continued, "I do not
wonder if some of these poor things owed their
advent to this world to ...."
(disgrace upon disgrace)!

Moloch-worship in Christendom as well! No
need of scouring through Indian mythologies to
create in one's imagination the horrors of Juggernaut. The heathen Ammonites sacrificed their
infants with distinct religious purposes; but
these night-hags. with no higher aim than those
"two dollars a piece." Assuredly you have
"heathens at your door." "Christendom is a
beastly land." So report some of my countrymen
who have travelled abroad, and saw only its dark
half. True, they are unfair; but as far as the
said beastliness goes, the impressions they have
received are correct. Heathendom cannot compete with Christendom in its beastliness as well.

But if Christendom's bad is so bad, how good
is its good! Seek through the length and breadth
of Heathendom, and see whether you can find one
John Howard to ornament its history of humanity.
My father, who, as I told you in my first chapter,
is a deep Confucian scholar, and whose admiration for the ancients of China is very strong, has
told me once and again, that from what he knows

of George Washington, Yao and Shun, upon
whom Confucius spent all his stock of eulogies,
were nothing compared with this liberator of
America; and I, with more knowledge of Washington than my father, can endorse his "historic
criticism" in full. Such combinations of heroism
and tenderness of heart, of ability and disinterest-
edness of purpose, of common-sense and enthusiasm in his religious conviction, as were those
of Oliver Cromwell, cannot be imagined of existence under non-Christian dispensation. We
have heard of our magnates hoarding millions, and
spending them upon temples, or feeding the poor
for their own "future's sake;" but a George Peabody or a Stephen Girard, who hoarded for the
sake of giving, and took delight in giving, is not
a phenomenon observable among heathens. And
not these select few only, but widely distributed
throughout Christendom, though necessarily hid-
den from view, are to be found what might be
specially named good men,—souls who love goodness for its own sake, and are bent toward doing
good, as mankind in general is bent toward doing
evil. How these souls, charily keeping themselves
from the view of the public, are striving to make
this world any bit better by their efforts and
prayers; how they often shed tears for the
wretchedness of the state of the people of whom
they read only in newspapers; how they lay upon
their hearts the welfare of the whole mankind;
and how willing they are to take part in the
work of ameliorating human misery and ignorance;—these I saw and witnessed with my own
eyes, and can testify to the genuine spirit that
underlies them all. These silent men are they,
who in their country's peril are the first to lay
down their lives in its service; who, when told of

a new mission enterprise in a heathen land, will deliver their railroad fares to the missionary who undertakes it, and return home tramping on their own feet, and praise God for their having done so; who in their big tearful hearts, understand all the mysteries of Divine Mercy, and hence are merciful toward all around them. No fierceness and blind zeal with these men, but gentleness, and cool calculation in doing good. Indeed, I can say with all truthfulness that I saw *good men* only in Christendom. Brave men, honest men, righteous men are not wanting in Heathendom, but I doubt whether *good men*,—by that I mean those men summed up in that one English word which has no equivalent in any other language: *Gentleman*,—I doubt whether such is possible without the religion of Jesus Christ to mould us. "The Christian, God Almighty's gentleman,"—he is a unique figure in this world, undescribably beautiful, noble, and lovable.

And not only are there such good men in Christendom, but their *power* over bad men is immense, considering the comparative scarcity of good men even in Christendom. This is another feature of Christendom, that goodness is more possible and more powerful there than in Heathendom. One Lloyd Garrison "friendless and unseen," and the freedom of a race began with him. One John B. Gough, and the huge intemperance begins to totter. Minority does not mean defeat with these people, though their Constitution seems to imply that effect. They are sure of their righteous cause, and sure of the national conscience, they feel sure to win the nation over to them. Rich men they fear and honor and admire, but good men, more. They are more proud of the goodness of Washington than of his bravery; of

Phillips Brooks than of Jay Gould. (Indeed, very many of them are really ashamed of the latter.) Righteousness with them is a power; and an ounce of righteousness goes against a pound of wealth, and often outweighs it.

Then their *national   conscience*,—by that I mean the sum total of the people's conscience as a nation,—how infinitely higher and purer than their average conscience! What as individuals they freely indulge in, they as a nation strongly protest against. I have heard it stated that many a blasphemer died a Christian death on the battlefields of the late Civil War in America; and I do not doubt the statement. The battle was one of principles, and not of honor and filthy lucre. They marched with a Christian aim in view: the liberation of an inferior race. Never in History has a nation gone into war with such an altruistic end in view. None but a Christian nation can go to such a war. Yet all were not Christians who went to this war.—Observe, too, how scrupulous these people are about the moral perfection of the men whom they choose as their Presidents. The men must not merely be able men, but moral men as well. No Richelieus or Mazarins can be their Presidents. Woe to that poor candidate, who in other respects is the fittest to rule; but a stain or two that mar his character has made him a failure. Morality does not usually count with statesmanship in Heathendom.—Why do they pursue the Mormons with so much rigor? Are not concubinage and polygamy of an "occult kind" actually practiced among these people? A strange inconsistency, you say. Strange, but to be admired. As a nation they cannot allow polygamy. Let those who practice it, do it secretly. The national conscience is not yet sharp enough to look after secrecies of this sort. But polygamy as an institution, under the sufferance and protection of the nation's laws, that neither Christians nor infidels will wink at. The Mormons must submit; else Utah shall not add one more star to the banner already spangled with so many bright and honorable stars.

The same national conscience that fosters all noble and worthy sentiments, keeps at bay all that are ignoble and unworthy. Broad daylight is denied to hags of all kinds. Such must put on garments of righteousness when they appear among the people; else they will be "lynched" by the very hags like themselves, and handed over to Oblivion and his angels. Mammon walks by the *laws* of righteousness. Honesty is believed to be the best policy, in politics as well as in other money-getting business. A man kisses his wife in society, whom he beats in his home. Gambling-houses go by the name of billiard rooms, and even the fallen angels by the title of "ladies." Saloons are all screened from outside views, and men drink in darkness, in evident shame of their evil habit. All very productive of the hypocrisies of the worst sort, you say. But does Virtue mean the licence of evils? I think not.

So then, this differencing of good from evil, of sky-loving larks from cave-dwelling bats, of sheep on the right hand from goats on the left,—this I consider to be a Christian state, the foretaste of that into which we are all going, the complete separation of the good from the bad. This Earth, though beautiful, was not originally meant as an angel-land. It was meant as a school to prepare us for some other places. This educational value of the Earth must not be lost sight of in our poor attempts to make it what it should be. Utilitarianism, Sentimental Christianity, and other shallow things, that, like the ancient Greeks, think this world to be gods' home, will stumble at Cromwells and other no-sweet prophets, because they cannot make all happy. In too many cases, "the greatest happiness to the greatest number" means just the reverse of a righteous and just government. I suppose nowhere under heaven are more "universal satisfactions" found than in African jungles upon the Congo or the Zambesi. That state is the best in which the best discipline of soul is possible, and hence the original aim of the creation of this Earth is best realized. When this is done, we all may quit this earth, and go, some of us to eternal bliss, and others to eternal no-bliss, and the Earth itself to its original elements, as a thing that has finished its business.

One more feature of Christendom before I cease to speak good things about it. There is one doctrine in Christianity upon which the recent Biology makes many after-dinner speeches;—I mean Resurrection. Let Renan and his disciples make whatever they please out of this doctrine; but the practical significance of this unique doctrine cannot be overlooked by "historical schools" of any turn of mind. Why is it that heathens in general go into decay so soon, but Christians in general know no decay whatever, but hope even in Death itself? Octogenarians still scheming for future as if they were still in twenties are objects of almost miraculous wonders with us heathens. We count men above forty among the old age, while in Christendom no man below fifty is considered to be fit for a position of any great responsibility. We think of rest and retirement as soon as our children come to age; and backed by the teaching of filial piety, we are entitled to lazy idleness, to be cared and caressed by the young generation. Judson, a missionary, after hardships of his life-time, exclaims he wants to live and work more, as he has eternity to rest. Victor Hugo in his eighty-four can say: "I improve every hour because I love this world as my fatherland. My work is only beginning. My monument is hardly above its foundation. I would be glad to see it mounting and mounting forever." Compare these with a Chinese poet Tao-Yuen-Ming who sought the solace of his old age in cups of liquor, or many of my own countrymen excusing themselves from the busy world as soon as grayness appears upon their heads. The godless physiology attributes all this to difference in diet, climate, and so forth; but the very fact that we too with our rice and monsoon can be other than what we used to be, calls for some other explanation than physiological.

I attribute the progressiveness of Christendom to its Christianity. Faith, Hope, and Charity, the three Life-angels that defy and shun Death and his angels, have worked upon it for the past nineteen hundred years, and have made it as we have it now.

> "Life mocks the idle hate
> Of his arch-enemy Death,—yea sits himself
> Upon the tyrant's throne, the sepulchre,
> And of the triumphs of his ghostly foe
> Makes his own nourishment."—Bryant.

Enormous yet though their sins are, these people have the power to overcome them. They have yet no sorrows which they think they cannot heal. Is not Christianity worth having if but for this power alone?

The *raison d' etre* of Christian mission? I think I have stated it already. It is the *raison d' etre* of Christianity itself. Said David Livingstone: "The spirit of missions is the spirit of our Master; the very genius of His religion. A diffusive philanthropy is Christianity itself. It requires perpetual propagation to attest its genuineness." Once it ceases to propagate, it ceases to live. Have you ever thought why it is that God leaves so large a part of the human race still in the darkness of heathenism? I think it is that your Christianity may live and grow by your efforts to diminish the darkness. One hundred and thirty-four millions of heathens yet! Thank God, there are still so many, for we need not like Alexander weep for the lack of the world to be conquered. Suppose God tells you to stay at home, and keep your purse-strings tight, and your hearts closed toward heathens. Think you you will thank Him for relieving you from useless obligations? If Christian mission is an obligation to you, for which you must have God's further blessings to reward you, and heathens' gratitude to keep your hearts warm, I believe you better cease to take any part in it, as neither God nor heathens get any good from you. "Woe is me if I preach not the Gospel." That was Apostle Paul. I believe, to him the greatest trial was *not* to be a missionary. With an expansive life in him, could he refrain himself from expanding into universal charity, which is Christian mission. I believe we better confess right honestly that we have no Christianity to speak of, than to grumble at "the difficulties of the station," "the insolence of heathens," and other cowardly things.

But why send missionaries to heathens when you have heathens enough in your own land?

You know this world is a unit, and the human race is one great family. This is what I read in my Christian Bible, though Patriotisms, Christian and otherwise, seem to deny this. You cannot make yourself perfect without making others perfect. An idea of a perfect Christendom in the midst of encircling heathenism is impossible. In Christianizing other peoples, you Christianize yourself. This is a philosophy abundantly illustrated by actual experiences.

Suppose you stop your foreign mission, and concentrate your whole energy upon home mission. What will you have? Many more striking conversions, many more homes freed from the curses of whisky, many more children decently clothed, no doubt. But withal what? Many more heresy-huntings, many more denominational back-bitings, with perhaps more Sunday-school excursions, and "Japanese marriages" in churches. I think you who have had Christianity now over eighteen hundred years have got over by this time that foolish and heathenish notion, that good done in one direction diminishes good to be done in others—Growth outside always means growth inside. You are troubled with some intestine lethargy. You go to your physician, and he medicates upon you nostrum after nostrum. But nothing heals you, and you begin to lose faith in your doctor. Finally you come to the true knowledge of your trouble. You turn your attention from inside; that is, you forget yourself, and go to some outside work, cultivation of cabbages, it may be. Then you begin to breathe freely, your bicep-muscles get bigger and firmer. Gradually you feel your trouble is gone, and you are now a stronger man than before. You healed yourself by reflex influences. You gave yourself upon cabbages, and cabbages healed you.

So with churches. Pruning with heresy-huntings, and medicating with New Theologies may never heal them. Nay, they may grow even worse. Now some wise men prescribe foreign missions to them. They take part in it, and they soon get interested in it. They have taken the whole world into their sympathy, and they feel themselves expanding by having done so. The new sympathy thus engendered calls up the old sympathy that has gone to sleep by heresy-trials and New Theology medicatings. What they failed to revive within them by spending themselves upon themselves, they now see returning to them by spending themselves upon other than themselves. You converted heathens, and heathens now reconvert you. Such is humanity, so intimately are you connected with the whole race. Pity the heathen? Do you *pity* your own brother in wretchedness? Are you not ashamed of him, and blame yourself for his wretched state? I believe this is the true philosophy of Christian mission; and missions started on any other basis than this are shows, plays, things to be criticized by their enemies, and disregarded by the very heathens to whom they are sent.

But you ask: Do you heathens like to have Christianity?

Yes, we sensible heathens do; and the insensible among us, though they throw stones at missionaries, and do other mischievous things upon them, as soon as they resume their sensibility, will see that they did wrong. Of course, we do not like many things that come under the name of Christianity. Hosts, surplices, compulsory prayer-books, theologies, unless they are absolute-

ly necessary to convey Christianity itself to us in
our present state of mental development, we do
desire to be spared from. We also like to have
no Americanianity and Anglicanianity imposed
upon us as Christianity. I hope none of us ever
threw stones at Christ Himself. If we did, we
stoned at the Almighty Throne itself, and we
shall have the Truth itself to condemn us. But
chide us not for throwing stones at missionaries
who in the name of Christ teach us their own
views,—theologies they call them,—and also their
own manners and customs, such as "free marriages," "woman's rights," and others, all more
or less objectionable to us. We do this for self-
preservation. You who tolerate Catholicism, but
not *Roman* Catholicism, who fling your pulpit addresses and newspaper editorials right at the
faces of Piuses and Leos for their interference in
your school and other public affairs, sympathize
with us in our protest against Americanism,
Anglicanism, and other foreign isms.

Then, when you come to us, come with strong
common sense. Do not believe the words of those
mission-circus men who tell you that a nation can
be converted in a day. There is no spiritual El
Dorado to be found upon this earth. Nowhere
can souls be converted by dozens and hundreds.
The same matter-of-fact world here as there. Men
do doubt, simulate, stumble, here as elsewhere.
I know some missionaries who preach to us as if
we were their own countrymen. They seem to
think that the method of Moody and Sankey that
goes so successfully with Americans and English-
men, should succeed equally well with Japanese
and Chinese. But Japanese and Chinese are *not*
Americans, as you well know. They had not their
childhood mothered with "Lord is my shepherd,"

"Now I lay me down to sleep," and other angelic melodies. They take as much delight in gong-bells as in Estey pipe-organs. They are "heathens," and you must teach them accordingly. But some preach Jesus Christ to them, give them a copy of New Testament, persuade them to be baptized, get their names enrolled in church-membership, and so have them reported to home-churches, and think that they are safe, and will go to heaven somehow. Perhaps they may, perhaps they may not. Hereditary influences, mental idiosyncracies, social environments, to say nothing of the same old Adamic propensity to sin in them, are not so readily conformable to the new and strange doctrines that are preached to them. Though we despise godless science, yet scienceless evangelization we do not put much value upon. I believe faith is wholly compatible with common-sense, and all zealous and successful missionaries have had this sense in abundance.

Come to us also, after fighting out Devils in your own souls. You know John Bunyan speaks of a reverend gentleman who had but very little experience with Devils. As he was not able to cure Bunyan's soul, so such as he cannot cure us heathens. "Born Christians," who have only heard of conversions, as "reports from a distance," cannot help us much in our death-struggles from Darkness to Light. I know a Quaker professor in America, who, when I told him of the doubts and difficulties that I had to overcome in my struggles Christward, said that he "could not very well see how that could have been, seeing that Christianity was so simple a thing as was contained in one monosyllable L-O-V-E." Only a monosyllable, but the Universe itself cannot contain it! An enviable man he. His ancestors had fought out

the battles for him. He came into this world un-
conscious of struggles, a ready-made Christian.
Like as a millionaire's son cannot comprehend the
miseries and strifes of a self-made man, so this
professor and many like him in Christendom cannot comprehend what we heathens have to fight
out in our souls before we get settled in peace in
that monosyllable. I advise such as he to stay at
home as professors, and not come to us as missionaries, for our complexities and sinuosities
may confound them, as their simplicities and
straight-cuttedness confound us. Indeed, those of
us who have had some earnest experiences with
Christianity, have found it not an altogether easy-
going, home-sweet-home, and peace-unto-all-men
affair. We have found it somewhat like poet
Bryant's Freedom,

"A bearded man,
Armed to the teeth, art thou; one mailed hand
Grasps the broad shield, and one the sword; thy
    brow
  Glorious in beauty though it be, is scarred
  With tokens of old wars; thy massive limbs
  Are strong with struggling."

We can appreciate "Pilgrim's Progress," but as
for that happy, happy, honey-moon style religion,
we know not what it is, but that it is not the
Christianity of the Crucified One. Heathenism
first subdued in your own soul; then you can subdue it right successfully in us.
    With your Christianity sifted from your own
isms, and your common-sense well sharpened (if
not sharp already), and best of all, with Devils
fought out in your own souls, I see no reason why
you should fail to do immense good to heathens.

Heathendom has had such missionaries (God be
thanked,) and it is crying for more. We soon take
no thought of them that they are strangers. Even
their very lack of our language is no barrier between them and us. Christianity is in their very
eyes. We feel it in their grasp of our hands. O
how they shine among us! Their very presence
dispels darkness. They need not preach unto us.
We will preach for them; only let them hold us
from behind. Rather one such than dozens and
hundreds of missionary adventurers and experi-
menters. "The work which an Archangel may
envy,—the work of preaching Christ to the heathen." Who but an archangel himself can engage
in this enviable work?

Yes, Christianity we do need. We need it not
so much to demolish our idols of wood and stone.
Those are innocent things compared with other
idols worshiped in Heathendom and elsewhere.
We need it to make our bad appear worse, and
our good appear better. It only can convince us
of sin; and convincing us of it, can help us to rise
above it, and conquer it. Heathenism I always
consider as a *tepid* state of human existence;—
it is neither *very* warm nor *very* cold. A lethargic
life is a weak life. It feels pain less; hence rejoices less. *De profundis* is not of heathenism.
We need Christianity to intensify us; to swear
fealty to our God, and enmity toward Devils. Not
a butterfly-life, but an eagle-life; not the dimuni-
tive perfection of a pink-rose, but the sturdy
strength of an oak. Heathenism will do for our
childhood, but Christianity alone for manhood.
The world is growing, and we with the world.
Christianity is getting to be a necessity with all
of us.

For fifty days I was upon the sea on my way

home. I sailed under the Southern Cross, saw the True Cross stand, and the False Cross fall. But think you not I was happy to see my dear ones so soon? Yes, happy in the sense that a soldier is happy, who dreams of conquests after encounter with his enemies. I was found by Him, and He girded me, and intimated to me that He would carry me whither I would not. Battles He assigned me in my own small sphere, and I was not to answer Nay. Alas I sought Him with much fightings. I found Him, and He ordered me at once to His battlefield! This the lot of one born in a soldier-family. Let me not murmur, but feel thankful.

May 16, Noon.—Clear, hazy in afternoon.— Came to the sight of my land about 10 A. M. Run 282 miles since yesterday noon. 63 miles more, and home.—Read 32nd chapter of Genesis. Much consoled by the thought that I am not worthy of the least of all the mercies which God hath shewed unto me during these years of my exile. His grace fills up all the vacancies left by the sad experiences of life. I know my life hath been guided by Him, and though I go with much fear and trembling to my homeland, I fear no evil, for He will still manifest more of Himself unto me.

Midnight. Reached home 9:30 P. M. Thank God I am here at last after travelling some 20,000 miles. The joy of the whole family knew no bounds. Perhaps it was the happiest

time my poor parents ever have had. Brother
and sister grown big, the former an active
little fellow, and the latter a quite nice girl.
Talked with father all night. Mother doesn't
care to learn about the world; she is only glad
that her son is safely at home. I thank God
for keeping my family all these years of my
absence from them. My prayer has been to
see my father in safety to tell him all that I
have seen and experienced.

"And Jacob said, O God of my father Abraham,
and God of my father Isaac, the Lord which saidst
unto me, Return unto thy country, and to thy
kindred, and I will deal well with thee. I am not
worthy of the least of all the mercies, and of all
the truth, which thou hast shewed unto thy servant; for with one staff I passed over the Jordan;
and now I am become two bands." (Gen. XXXII,
9, 10.) This the state of one whom the Lord liketh
to honor. Jacob had in Haran all that he had
sought after and prayed for: Leah and Rachel,
children, sheep. I too, a poor servant of His, had
in Christendom all that I had sought after and
prayed for. Not indeed the kind with which Jacob
was blessed. Indeed, so strait was my condition
in this respect that I had only 75 cents left in my
pocket after my roamings over 20,000 miles of land
and sea. My mental capital too, which I carried
home was inconsiderable compared with that
which is usually brought back by my countrymen
of my own age and circumstance. Science, Medicine, Philosophy, Divinity,—not a sheepskin of
this kind had I in my trunk to please my parents

as my present to them. But I had what I wished
to have, even — —, "unto the Jews a stumblingblock, and unto the Greeks foolishness." True,
I did not find it in Christendom in the way I had
expected; i. e. I had not picked it up in streets,
or even in churches or in theological seminaries;
but in ways various and contrarious, I had it
nevertheless, and I was satisfied. This then my
present to my parents and countrymen, whether
they like it or not. This the Hope of human souls,
this the Life of nations. No philosophy or divinity
can take *its* place in the history of mankind. "I
am not ashamed of the gospel of Christ; for it is
the power of God unto salvation to every one
that believeth, to the Jew first, and also to the
Greek."

I reached my home late in evening. There upon
a hill, enclosed by Cryptomeria hedge, stood my
paternal cottage. "Mamma," I cried as I opened
the gate, "your son is back again." Her lean
form, with many more marks of toil upon it, how
beautiful! The ideal beauty that I failed to recog-
nize in the choices of my Delaware friend, I found
again in the sacred form of my mother. And my
father, the owner of a twelfth part of an acre upon
this spacious globe,—he is a right hero too, a just
and patient man. Here is a spot then which I may
call my own, and by which I am chained to this
Land and Earth. Here my Home and my Battlefield as well, the soil that shall have my service,
my prayers, my life, free.

The day after my arrival at home, I received
an invitation to the principalship of a *Christian*
college said to have been started by *heathens*. A
singular institution this, unique in the history of
the world. Shall I accept it?

But here this book must close. I have told you

how I became a convert to Christianity. Should my life prove eventful enough, and my readers not tired of my ways of telling. I have in mind another book of later experiences.

FINIS.

Bible Readings.

Notes and Suggestions for Bible Readings. By S. R. Briggs and J. H. Elliott. *45th thousand.* 8vo, paper, 50c.; flexible cloth, 75c.; cloth.................... . ... $1.00

    Acknowledged to be the very best help for Bible readings in print. Over six hundred outlines of Bible readings by many of the most eminent Bible students of the day.

New Notes for Bible Readings. By S. R. Briggs. With memoir by Rev. J. H. Brookes, D.D. 8vo, flexible cloth, 75c.; cloth, 1.00

    " The readings are practical helpful, full of suggestiveness, and bring out the most important points and truths in the subjects on which they are based. It is, in fact, the best thing of the kind we have seen."—*The Christian at Work.*

Scriptural Outlines by Books and Themes. By William G. Carr. 12mo, cloth..... .... .75

    " They are adapted to the Student of the Sacred Scriptures, in his private work at home, or in his public work as a Bible Reader. They will inevitably stimulate devotion and a knowledge of the Word."—*The Golden Rule.*

Flashes from the Lighthouse of Truth; or, Bible Readings on the First Three Chapters of the First Epistle to the Church at Thessalonica. By Rev. F. E. Marsh. 12mo, cloth...... ... 1.00

    " Has a distinct mission and deserves wide popularity."—*Ram's Horn.*

The Open Secret; or, The Bible Explaining Itself. A Series of Practical Bible Readings. By Hannah Whitall Smith, author of " The Christian's Secret of a Happy Life." 12mo, cloth... 1.00

Bible Briefs; or, Outline Themes for Scripture Students. By Geo. C. and E. A. Needham. 12mo, cloth................. 1.00

Broken Bread for Serving Disciples. A Companion to " Bible Briefs." By Geo. C. and E. A. Needham. 12mo, cloth.... 1.00

    " We have looked through this book with pleasure and commend it heartily. It is a good sign that such works are in demand."—*The N. Y. Evangelist.*

Gold from Ophir. Bible Readings, Original and Selected. By J. E. Wolfe. Introduction by Rev. J. H. Brookes, D.D. 8vo, cloth..................... .... 1.25

    " A warehouse of pulpit and platform furniture ready for use. Everything is condensed and analyzed, so that there is not a line to spare."—*C. H. Spurgeon.*

Ruth, the Moabitess. Gleanings in the Book of Ruth. by Henry Moorhouse. 12mo, paper, 20c.; cloth .... .40

Bible Readings. By Henry Moorhouse. 12mo, paper, 30c.; cloth..... .... .60

    ***See also Introductory Studies, Works of Reference, and Commentaries.**

Bible Readers Hints.

Hints on Bible Study. A Symposium. By Dr. Clifford, Professors Drummond and Elmslie, Revs. Moule, Horton, Meyer, Waller, Berry, and Dawson. 12mo, cloth..................$ .50

Bible Difficulties and How to Meet Them. A Symposium. *Fourth Thousand.* 12mo, cloth............................ .50
CONTENTS—Inspiration, by Dr. Clifford—The Bible and Science, by Rev. F. Ballard—The Incarnation, by Rev. Prebendary Gordon Calthrop—Miracles, by Rev. R. F. Horton—The Atonement, by the Rev. J. Reid Howatt—The Reliability of the Gospels, by Rev. A. R. Buckland—The Resurrection, by Rev. F. B. Meyer—The Trinity in Unity, by Rev. Dr. Hiles Hitchens.

Among Many Witnesses. A Book for Bible Students. By M. B. Williams. 12mo, cloth.............................. .... 1.00

Bible Helps for Busy Men. By A. C. P. Coote. 12mo, paper, 30c.; cloth... .60

Red Letter Readings. By Miss Bessie B. Tyson. 12mo, paper, 25c.; cloth........ .... .50

Pegs of Preachers—Points for Workers. By Charles Inglis. 12mo, cloth........... .. .. .75
"Calculated to be helpful guides to any who may wish to avail themselves of them."—*The Christian Intelligencer.*

Supplemental Bible Studies. By Rev. H. T. Sell. 8vo, paper, net, 25c.; cloth..net, .50
This book meets the demand for a short and comprehensive course of study upon the Structure, Geography, History, and Institutions of the Bible. There are three outline maps and a blackboard outline for every lesson.
"Mr. Sell has had the rare good fortune to hit upon the doing of exactly the kind of thing sorely needed to be done, and he has done it well."—*The Advance.*

A Pocket Concordance to the Scriptures. By Rev. John Brown. 32mo, cloth.... .... net, .25
Printed on good paper and substantially bound. A ready companion for the traveler.

4,000 Scripture Questions with Answers. 16mo, paper. 25c.; cloth .... .50

Symbols and System in Bible Readings. By Rev. W. F. Crafts. 16mo, paper.. .25

How to Mark your Bible. By Mrs. Stephen Menzies. With prefatory note by D. L. Moody. 8vo, paper, 35c.; cloth.... .75
"An almost inexhaustible number of suggestions for marginal notes and markings. It is a book every Christian worker will do well to have among his Bible helps."—*The Young Men's Era.*

How to Study the Bible. By D. L. Moody. *Revised.* 16mo, paper, 10c.; flexible cloth .. .. .15

₊ *See also Introductory Studies, Works of Reference, and Commentaries.*

Works of Reference.

Topical Outlines of Bible Themes. An Illustrative Scripture Reference Book, and Selected Concordance to the more Important Passages of Scripture. By Rev. G. S. Bowes. 12mo, cloth....... .. .. $1.50

The Treasury of Scripture Knowledge. Consisting of *Five Hundred Thousand* Scripture References and Parallel Passages, and numerous Illustrative Notes. 8vo, cloth..... .... 2.00
" Bible students who desire to compare scripture with scripture will find the ' Treasury ' to be a better help than any other book of which I have any knowledge."—*R. R. McBurney, General Sec'y, Y. M. C. A., New York.*

The Bible Text Cyclopedia. A Complete Classification of Scripture Texts in the form of an Alphabetical List of Subjects. By Rev. James Inglis. 8vo, cloth.................... .. .. 1.75
" More sensible and convenient, and every way more satisfactory than any book of the kind we have ever known. We know of no other work comparable with it, in this department of study."—*The Sunday School Times.*

Cruden's Complete Concordance. Large 8vo, cloth........ 1.00
Half-leather, sprinkled edges.. .... 1.50
Half-roan, cloth sides, gilt edges.......................net, 2.50

The Comprehensive Concordance to the Holy Scriptures. Based on the Authorized Version. By Rev. J. B. R. Walker. 922 pages, 8vo, cloth........ .... 2.00

Smith's Dictionary of the Bible: Its Antiquities, Biography, Geography, and Natural History. With numerous illustrations and maps. *Worker's Edition.* 8vo, cloth................ 1.50
This work contains over 500 engravings, and is a complete guide to the pronunciation and signification of scriptural names; the solution of difficulties of interpretation, authority and harmony. Also, a history and description of Biblical customs, manners, events, places, persons, animals, plants, minerals, etc. It is a most complete encyclopedia of Biblical information.

Topical Text Book. A Scripture Text Book for the Use of Ministers, Teachers, Visitors, etc. Parts I. and II. in one volume. 16mo, cloth.. . ... .60
" I find one of the very best ways to study the scriptures is to study *Topically.*"—*D. L. Moody.*

The Works of Flavius Josephus. Translated by William Whiston, A.M. With life, portrait, notes, and index. *A New Edition in Clear Type.* 8vo, cloth............. . ... 1.50

A Complete Dictionary of Synonyms and Antonyms; or, Synonyms and Words of Opposite Meaning. By Rev. Samuel Fallows, A.M. 16mo, cloth........................ ...... 1.00

Revell's Biblical Wall Atlas. Prepared by T. Ruddiman Johnston, F.R.G.S. Eight large sheets containing thirty Maps and Plans. Mounted on spring rollers and set in handsome hardwood case......... ....net, 40.00
Folded style, enclosed in portfolios .. ..net, 30.00
Complete descriptive circular on application.

Revell's Imperial Globe Atlas of Modern and Ancient Geography. Containing 53 imperial quarto maps, with an index of 20,000 names. Large 4to, 12x14, cloth....,,,,,,,,,,,,,,,,,,,net, 1.00

Addresses, Sermons, and Essays.

Essential Christianity. By Rev. Hugh Price Hughes. 12L)0, cloth,..$1.25

Fully sustains the reputation of this famous London preacher.

Ten Minute Sermons. By Rev. W. Robertson Nicoll, D.D. 1:mo, cloth, gilt top...................................... 1.50

Brilliant sermonettes by the editor of "The Expositor's Biʋle "

Three Gates on a Side, and Other Sermons. By Rev. Charles H. Parkhurt. 12mo, cloth, gilt top...................... 1.25

" Dr. Parkhurst is certainly a preacher of unusual power, and a thinker of marked originality."—*The Churchman.*

The Ideal of Humanity in the Old Times and New. By Prof. John Sʌuart Blackie, author of " On Self Culture." 12mo, cloth 1.00

" Fresh, forcible and practical. In close and helpful touch with everyday life."—*The Congregationalist.*

Sermons by the Rev. John McNeill. Vols. I., II. and III., each containing 26 Sermons. 12mo, cloth, each................ 1.50

" The Rev. John McNeil' has a firm hold of Gospel truth, a clear mind, and a peculiar and graphic method of expressing sound convictions."—*Rev. John Hall, D.D.*

Twelve Sermons by the late Eugene Bersier, D.D., of l'Eglise de l'Etoile, Paris. Translated by Mrs. Alexander Waugh. With portrait. 12mo, cloth...................................... 1.25

" We have read these sermons with very great delight. Bersier was a preacher of eloquence, force, and profit."—*The Independent.*

Princeton Sermons. Chiefly by Professors in Princeton Theological Seminary. 12mo, cloth............................. 1.50

The contributors are President Patten, and Professors Green, Hodge, Warfield, Aiken, Murray, and Davis.
"Scholarly, vigorous, and practical."—*The Congregationalist.*
" Coiᴎ from the royal mint of the King of Heaven."—*The N. Y. Observer.*

Pacific Coast Pulpit. Sermons by Representative Preachers (··) the Pacific Coast. With 17 portraits. 12mo, cloth.......... 2.ᴖᴖ

Divine Balustrades, and other Sermons. By Rev. R. S. MacArthur, D.D. 12mo, cloth................................. 1.25

" Marked by mental precision, and an atmosphere of spirituality that is decidedly refreshing."—*The Golden Rule.*

Sermons. By Rev. John A. Boardus, D.D. 12mo, cloth..... 1.00

Baccalaureate and Other Addresses. By Rev. E. A. Tanner, D.D., late President of Illinois College. 12mo, cloth....... 1.50

⁎ *See also Moody, Meyer, Herron, Stalker, and Spurgeon.*

For Evangelistic Work.

Grace and Truth under Twelve Different Aspects. By W. P. Mackay, M.A. *60th thousand.* 12mo, paper, 35c.; cloth...$ .75
Abridged Edition, 12mo, paper........................... .15
   "I know of no book in print better adapted to aid in the work of him who would be a winner of souls, or to place in the hands of the unconverted."—*D. L. Moody.*

Steps to Christ. By Mrs. E. G. White. *40th thousand.* 12mo, cloth .... .75
   "Plain and practical, and calculated to explain away the difficulties that beset the pathway of not a few Christians,"—*The N. Y. Observer.*

Regeneration. By Prof. George Nye Boardman. 12mo, cloth, .75
   "Possessed of a devout mind and clear views of the truth, apt to teach and writing in a style that is clear and perspicuous, Dr. Boardman does service to the truths of which he treats."—*The N. Y. Observer.*

Life in a Look. By Rt. Rev. M. S. Baldwin, D.D. 16mo, flexible cloth... .25
   "It is below its value to say that it is worth its weight in gold."—*The Truth.*

The Blood of Jesus. By Rev. W. Reid. Edited by Rev. E. P. Hammond. 16mo, paper, 10c.; cloth...................... .25

How to Bring Men to Christ. By Rev. R. A. Torrey, Supt. of the Chicago Bible Institute. 16mo, cloth................. .75
   "A plain, simple, forcible treatise, judicious and practical. which all Christians will do well to study."—*The Congregationalist.*

The Worker's Weapon. Its Perfection, Authority, Study, and Use. By Rev. John Henry Elliott. 18mo, flexible cloth... .50
   By the joint author of Briggs' and Elliott's popular "Notes and Suggestions for Bible Readings."

Bible Manual. For Christian Workers, Inquirers and Young Converts. By. Rev. Alex. Patterson. 12mo, paper, net, 15c.; flexible cloth..net, .25
   Scripture Texts, arranged under classified headings, with Index and Hints to Workers.

Lessons for Christian Workers. Containing a large number of Plans, Methods and Hints for effective Christian Service. By Rev. C. H. Yatman. Long 18mo, leatherette covers....... .25

The Christian Workers Hand-book. By F. T. Pierson. Long 18mo, paper.. .25

Furnishing for Workers. A Manual for Christian Workers. By Rev. L. W. Munhall. 32mo, flexible leather........net, .25

Words for the Anxious. A Worker's Hand-book. By M. B. Williams. 32mo, flexible leather.......................... .25

See also Smith, Meyer, Moody, and Pierson.

For Work Among Children.

Children's Meetings, and How to Conduct Them; with Lessons, Outlines, Diagrams, Music, and Helpful Suggestions. By Lucy J. Rider and Nellie M. Carman. Introduction by Rev. J. H. Vincent, D.D. 12mo, paper, net, 50c.; cloth.........net, $1.00
"It evidently aims to teach the leader to talk with children rather than to them; to encourage the memorizing of Bible verses; and to make use of the lessons from nature, as did the Master. Sunday School teachers as well as the leaders of children's meetings may find here many useful hints."—*The Golden Rule.*

Attractive Truths in Lesson and Story. By Mrs. A. M. Scudder. Introduction by Rev. F. E. Clark, President Y. P. S. C. E. 12mo, cloth.. 1.25
A series of outline lessons, with illustrative stories, for Junior Christian Endeavor Societies, Children's Meetings, and Home Teaching.
"The selections are excellent, the suggestions useful, and the ideas eminently practical."—*The Christian Advocate* (N.Y.)

The Conversion of Children. By Rev. E. P. Hammond. 12mo, paper, 25c.; cloth... .75

Short Talks to Young Christians on the Evidences. By Rev. C. O. Brown. 18mo, paper, 30c.; cloth..................... .50

Foundation Stones. A Series of Lectures to the Young. By Rev. Robert F. Coyle. 12mo, cloth....................... 1.00
A valuable work on the fundamental evidences of our Christian faith.

Talks to Children. By Rev. T. T. Eaton, D.D. Introduction by Rev. John A. Broadus, D.D. 12mo, cloth, gilt top......... 1.00
"They reproduce Scripture history in the terms of modern life, and give it both a vivid setting before the youthful imagination, and a firm grip on the youthful conscience."—*The Independent.*

Newton's Sermons to Children. 9 vols., 12mo, cloth, each, 1.00
Send for list of Rev. Richard Newton's Sermons to Children.

At Mother's Knee. The Mother's Holy Ministry with Her Children in the Home. By Rev. J. M. P. Otts, D.D. With appropriate design on side. 12mo, cloth................. 1.00
Written for the profit and pleasure of children 'and all who love them. Beautiful alike in conception and execution.

Before He Is Twenty. Five perplexing phases of the Boy Question considered. With portraits of the authors. 16mo, cloth, gilt top.." .... .75
The ",phases" and authors are:
The Father and His Boy .... Robert J. Burdette
When He Decides .... Frances Hodgson Burnett
The Boy in the Office ....Edward W. Bok
His Evenings and Amusements .... Mrs. Burton Harrison
Looking Toward a Wife .... Mrs. Lyman Abbott

The Science of Motherhood. By Hannah Whitall Smith. 12mo, leatherette boards... .35

A Message to Mothers. By Rev. B. Fay Mills. 12mo, paper, .25

Living Papers.

Living Papers on Present Day Themes. On Subjects of Christian Evidence, Doctrine and Morals. 10 vols., 12mo, cloth, each.......................... $1.00
The set, boxed............................. 10.00

> An authorized American reprint of a most remarkable collection of sixty papers by the ablest writers, among whom are the distinguished authorities mentioned in connection with the single volumes named below. Complete list of authors and subjects on application.

The Argument for Christianity. Being Vol. XI, "Living Papers." By Principal Cairns, Prof. Blaikie and Rev. Drs. Kaufman, Lewis, Chapman, and Slater. 12mo, cloth.................................... 1.00

SPECIAL VOLUMES.

Containing papers selected from the " Living Papers " Series.

The Non-Christian Religions of the Age. By Sir W. Muir, Drs. Legge, Murray Mitchell, and H. B. Reynolds. 12mo, cloth... .... 1.00

Christ the Central Evidence of Christianity, and other Papers. By Principal Cairns. 12mo, cloth.. 1.00

The Higher Criticism. By the Dean of Canterbury, Dean Howson, Principal Wace, and Professors Bruce and Godet. 12mo, cloth................. .... 1.00

Man in Relation to the Bible and Christianity. By Prebendary Row, Canon Rawlinson, Professors Macalister, W. G. Blaikie, Radford Thomson, F. Pfaff, S. R. Pattison, Sir William Dawson and Rev. W. S. Lewis. 12mo, cloth 1.40

The Non-Christian Philosophies of the Age. By Professors Blaikie, Radford Thomson, Porter and Iverach, and Rev. W. F. Wilkinson. 12mo, cloth,......... 1.40

Prophecy.

Ecce Venit; or, Behold He Cometh. By Rev. A. J. Gordon, D.D.
12mo, paper, net, 50c.; cloth, gilt top.....................$1.25
"It is the fruit of many years' study of this question by a
mind rich in its own native equipment, and further enriched by
study and by constant communion with the loftiest and most inspiring themes."—*The Standard.*

Jesus is Coming. By W. E. Blackstone. *70th thousand. New
and Enlarged Edition.* 16mo, paper, 15c.; cloth........... .50

Studies in Eschatology; or, The Thousand Years in both Testaments, with Supplementary Discussions upon Symbolical Numbers, the Development of Prophecy and its Interpretation
concerning Israel, the Nations, the Church, and the Kingdom,
as seen in the Apocalypses of Isaiah, Ezekiel, Daniel, Christ and
John. By Rev. Nathaniel West, D.D. 8vo. cloth......... 2.00

Why We Expect Jesus Now. By John Mason. 16mo, paper,
25c.; cloth.. .60

The Lord's Return, and Kindred Truth. By Rev. L. W. Munhall, M.A. 12mo. cloth................................. 1.00
"We know of no work better suited to place in the hands of
one who has not fully made up his mind on this important question."—*The Episcopal Recorder.*

The Second Coming of Christ. By D. L. Moody. 16mo, paper .10

The Blessed Hope; or, The Glorious Coming of the Lord. By
Willis Lord, D.D. 12mo, cloth,........................... 1.00

Plan of the Ages. With Chart. By George C. Needham. 12mo,
paper.. .... .25
Seven thousand years of human history—from creation to
consummation.

Lectures on the Book of Revelation. By W. Lincoln. 12mo
paper, 50c., cloth,..................................... 1.00

Prophetic Studies of the International Prophetic Conference
upon the Near Coming of the Lord, and kindred Topics and
Events; together with their Practical Application as an Incen-
tive to Evangelistic and Mission Work, and Personal Consecra-
tion. 8vo, paper, net, 50c.; cloth....... ....net, .75

What is Maranatha? By G. W. Gillings. 16mo, paper.... .20

Jew and Gentile. A Report of the Chicago Conference of Jews
and Christians to Consider their Mutual Relations. 8vo, paper,
50c.; cloth.. .75

The Jewish Problem, Its Solution; or, Israel's Present and
Future. By David Baron. Introduction by Rev. A. T. Pierson. D.D, 12mo, cloth.................................... .60

*** See also *Brookes.*

BV3457
U3

ImTheStory.com

Lightning Source UK Ltd.
Milton Keynes UK
UKOW05f1915160517
301349UK00016B/601/P